Suicide

First published in 2015 by
Liberties Press
140 Terenure Road North | Terenure | Dublin 6W
T: +353 (1) 905 6072| W: libertiespress.com | E: info@libertiespress.com

Trade enquiries to Gill & Macmillan Distribution
Hume Avenue | Park West | Dublin 12
T: +353 (1) 500 9534 | F: +353 (1) 500 9595 | E: sales@gillmacmillan.ie

Distributed in the United Kingdom by
Turnaround Publisher Services
Unit 3 | Olympia Trading Estate | Coburg Road | London N22 6TZ
T: +44 (0) 20 8829 3000 | E: orders@turnaround-uk.com

Distributed in the United States by
International Publishers Marketing
22841 Quicksilver Dr | Dulles, VA 20166
T: +1 (703) 661-1586 | F: +1 (703) 661-1547 | E: ipmmail@presswarehouse.com

ISBN: 978-1-909718-29-6
2 4 6 8 10 9 7 5 3 1

A CIP record for this title is available from the British Library.

Cover design by Karen Vaughan – Liberties Press
Internal design by Liberties Press

This book reflects the views of the authors, and not those of any organisation.

Suicide

A Modern Obsession

Derek Beattie and Dr Patrick Devitt

*This book is dedicated to all those who have died by suicide
and to their families*

Table of Contents

Acknowledgements

We would like to acknowledge the patience and assistance of our friends and families. Thanks to those who gave up their time for interviews: Professor Ella Arensman, Dr Justin Brophy, Rene Duignan, Joan Freeman, Dr Declan Murray and Dr Dermot Walsh. Carl O'Brien of the *Irish Times* was especially helpful and we are grateful to those families who opened up their grief to Carl in such a public way. Sean O'Keeffe of Liberties Press has remained enthusiastic since we first approached him with our idea for this book, and he has been a constant encouragement. The professionalism and guidance of our editor, Sam Tranum, and all the staff at Liberties have been invaluable. This work has also benefitted from the advice of Dr Selena Pillay, Stephen Shannon and a number of other colleagues.

Foreword

By Dr Dermot Walsh

I am delighted to provide a foreword to this contribution to an issue that has become increasingly the subject of debate and media attention in Ireland in recent years. Such consideration, not all of it well informed, is understandable, as suicide is a major cause of mortality, particularly among young males, and therefore constitutes a significant public health problem. This book brings examination and critical appraisal to bear on the issue of suicide internationally and within Ireland. It includes an historical review of the matter, from antiquity onwards, looking at how the taking of one's life was perceived in widely different cultural settings. It also reviews causes and examines preventive endeavours. It does not neglect the distress of those – family and others – affected by each suicide and the provisions necessary to ease their pain. And it includes some evocative case histories.

Within the narrower domestic focus of Ireland, issues relating to suicide, its public perception, and indigenous preventive strategies are examined. In this context, the main interest from an Irish point of view is the original, perhaps controversial focus it brings to bear on the effort expended on prevention, grappling with the issue in the recent Irish context.

During the nineteenth century, the number of recorded Irish suicides was extremely low in the European context and, despite a moderate official increase before the First World War, it fell away again in the post-war decades. It took some time to establish, on a scientific basis, an approximately accurate rate, as distinct from the official rate as returned by the reports of the Registrar General compiled from coroner's determinations as submitted to the Central Statistics Office (CSO). Critical examinations of coroner's and hospital records of violent deaths revealed that the 'true' rate of suicidal death was at least twice as high as represented in CSO data. Nonetheless, there were reasons for believing that, even allowing for a revised death rate more accurately representing the real situation, Irish suicide rates were still relatively low in the international context.

Then, in the third and fourth quarters of the twentieth century, suicide numbers and rates in Ireland began to rise – according to both official and unofficial numbers – although the gap between these two assessments had by then closed considerably. By late-century, however, while Ireland's overall suicide rate was still in the middle of the European range, the rate for its young males had increased worryingly and was greater than the rates for young males in most other jurisdictions. These suicides were quite often impulsive and carried out in the context of alcohol, by young males not generally perceived as suffering from mental illness in the formal sense, despite the claims by researchers that most suicides occur in persons with established mental disorders. This increase then flattened out in the early years of the twenty-first century. While long-term trends were clear, year-on-year and regional variations within Ireland were also less meaningful because of the small numbers involved.

Youth suicide in Ireland became an issue catalysing considerable popular and political preoccupation with prevention.

Organisations active in prevention, small and large, flourished and prospered and competed for considerable resources to pursue their activities. From the 1990s to early 2000s national policy documents were produced advocating numerous intervention typologies. And, more recently, the Health Service Executive (HSE) has identified suicide prevention as one of its major service programmes in mental health. Simultaneously, data has been gathered on persons presenting to emergency departments of general hospitals describing the occurrence of self-harm, and the characteristics of such persons, most of whom, in fulfilment of HSE policy, are evaluated by dedicated nursing staff.

This book points out that much of this activity, some of it resting on inspirational rather than scientific insights, and little of it evaluated in any critical manner, may be of doubtful benefit. Suicide prevention, whether on a population or high-risk basis, is challenging – as this book points out. Searching for causal relationships in short-run and unstable data can thwart many a research endeavour, given the rarity of suicide and the wide prevalence of perceived risk indicators. But this publication reaches beyond the domestic scene and examines the relationships between international impacts such as economic recessions, and cultural influences.

A nation has the responsibility to preserve human life, including by preventing suicide. This book highlights the difficulty of this moral and political obligation, given the heterogeneity and complexity of the roots of the tragedy that is suicide.

1.
Introduction

In July 2012, Ireland's then minister for health, Dr James Reilly, described suicide as 'a tragedy that we are constantly working to prevent'. Kathleen Lynch TD, minister of state with responsibility for mental health, reaffirmed the government's commitment to preventing suicide in September 2014 when she stressed that all of the cabinet was very concerned about the high rate of suicide in Ireland. Yet some suicide-prevention campaigners claim that the government is not doing enough to tackle the problem.

It is difficult to level the same charge at civil society and ordinary Irish people. In a country with a population of just over 4.5 million, there are around 400 organisations dedicated to preventing suicide. Typically, these organisations have developed as well-meaning local responses to the tragedy of suicide.

The Irish media are fascinated with the high incidence of suicide among young males in the country and eager to offer suggestions on how this problem should best be addressed. In a 2014 article coinciding with World Suicide-Prevention Day, Arlene Harris of the *Irish Times* suggested that:

> Society has realised that, in order to reach out and help people who are struggling on the brink, the topic needs to be discussed openly, and those who are suffering need to know there is no shame in feeling despair.[1]

Interest in suicide crosses many cultures. A Japanese book, the *Complete Manual of Suicide*, contains detailed descriptions and analyses of different suicide methods and has sold more than a million copies. The South Korean government is so concerned about the prevalence of Internet content promoting and encouraging suicide that a hundred people are employed there to monitor the Internet for such material. Google generated around 19 million results using the word 'suicide' in November 2014.

So suicide is clearly a topic of enormous public concern and interest. The question is why. Though it may be difficult for those who have lost a friend or relative to suicide to comprehend, it still remains a relatively rare event. In most developed countries, the number of suicide deaths is just about comparable to the number of road-traffic fatalities. While there is significant interest in reducing mortality from road-traffic accidents, the public are not as feverishly gripped by the topic. Why is there apparently more interest in suicide than in road-traffic accidents?

The roots of what we describe as the 'modern obsession'[2] with suicide can be traced back to the nineteenth century. Suicide started to captivate the public imagination when rates increased in many Western countries in the second half of the nineteenth century, and mortality from many of the other main causes of death decreased.[3] Less-hostile societal attitudes to suicide were also a legacy of the Enlightenment and further fed the development of this fascination. The Christian prohibition on voluntary death, as well as the harsh treatments of the bodies of suicide victims, had ensured that for centuries before this, there had been a huge social taboo around the topic.

Our preoccupation with suicide does not mean that the stigma surrounding the issue has entirely disappeared in the twenty-first century. Introduce suicide into a conversation at any social occasion and a wide range of reactions can be expected, from silence to sadness, from a defence of the right to suicide to outrage that more is not being done to curb the problem. The well-known anti-psychiatrist Thomas Szasz bemoaned the fact that English has only one word to describe self-inflicted death, one we hate to utter.[4] It is not uncommon for families who have lost relatives to suicide to encounter negative reactions. People may avoid speaking to them, or change the subject when a bereaved family member wants to speak about the deceased.

The continued existence of a stigma does not hinder – and, in fact, may explain – some of the intense interest in suicide, much as banning a film can entice more people to see it. There is certainly sustained media interest in voluntary death, often reflecting what consultant psychiatrist Dr Justin Brophy, the chairman of the Irish Association of Suicidology, has described as 'a peddling of tabloid interest in human misery and despair'.[5] Media guidelines that emphasise the need for sensitivity when reporting on such situations are regularly ignored. For example, the reporting on the March 2014 suicide of fashion designer L'Wren Scott saw a number of British tabloids fascinated with capturing photographs of her grieving partner, Rolling Stones singer Mick Jagger, reach new lows.

Though suicide is relatively rare, there are still around 800,000 suicides around the world every year. Millions are left behind to wonder why these were not prevented. Often, they grapple with understanding why their loved ones killed themselves, and with their perceived roles in the deaths, wondering why they did not pick up on the signs. The effects of suicide are far-reaching and extend to friends, peers and work colleagues.

Health professionals and those working in crisis services can also be deeply traumatised. Some start to question their own competence or resolve to completely avoid treating suicidal clients in the future. This burden can be aggravated by grieving families, who may actively blame professionals for not averting the death. After a patient's suicide, there will usually be detailed reviews of their care. Such appropriate and important avenues for learning sadly often foster a culture of blame. No wonder, then, that mental-health services are obsessed with suicide, attempting to predict and prevent it, usually through psychiatric intervention.

★

The nineteenth-century French sociologist Emile Durkheim defined suicide as 'all cases of death resulting directly or indirectly from a positive or negative act of the victim himself, which he knows will produce this result.'[6] Albert Camus, the twentieth-century existentialist philosopher, believed it was the only really serious philosophical problem. According to existentialism, we determine the definitions and directions of our own lives bearing in mind that our lives are trivial in the greater scheme of things. In this context, Camus apparently once posed the question, 'Should I kill myself or have a cup of coffee?'[7] Jennifer Hames and others, in a 2012 academic journal article, wrote about what they called the 'high-place phenomenon', a sudden urge to jump from a high place, experienced by both those with suicidal thoughts and those who have none – they could, in one simple act, eliminate a life, with all its so-called meaning, complexity and importance.[8]

Suicide can be viewed from a multitude of other perspectives, in addition to the sociological and philosophical. These include religious, psychological, political, cultural, public health and even biochemical perspectives. Suicide goes back to the origins of civilisation; it seems always to have existed. A rich history of suicide among the ancient Greeks and Romans can be unearthed, which mainly focuses on the deaths of aristocratic men.

The father of psychoanalysis, Sigmund Freud, believed suicide was the result of a murder instinct turned inwards, but the view of mental-health professionals that it is predominantly caused by mental illness has been a much more enduring theoretical view. Statistical peaks can be found in unmarried men and in older men. In some countries, there is a high prevalence of suicide among young men. In Ireland, it is the leading cause of death among males between the ages of fifteen and twenty-four.

Some historical suicides were regarded as noble, honourable and brave – especially when conducted in the context of battle. The 'honourable death' remains a source of great pride in some Eastern countries, especially Japan. In other parts of the world, however, suicides are almost always seen as tragedies. The loss of a young person in their prime is regarded as a terrible waste and is a huge emotional blow to their friends and family – and especially to their parents, who reared them and cannot have expected that they would be predeceased by their offspring.

It is not surprising that great effort is expended in attempting to understand the motivations of those who take their own lives. Through greater understanding, it is hoped that we can ultimately identify the means of prevention. The isolation of specific causes for a particular suicide is a very difficult task because, frequently, many factors are involved in the decision.

There are a number of factors known to be associated with suicide. Cultural factors are relevant and account for the variation in rates between different countries and within countries. A high rate of alcohol and substance abuse and dependence is also associated with suicide. Individuals suffering with serious mental illness are more likely to kill themselves. Certain professions are known to have a higher prevalence of suicide – for example, doctors, dentists, police officers and soldiers.

Other factors also impinge on this topic. We will explore:

- Whether suicidal behaviour is itself a sign of a mental illness;

- What role impulsivity plays, as some suicides appear to have no obvious causes;

- The impacts of the economy and media exposure;

- Questions of morality – whether suicide is wrong and if there can be such a thing as a rational suicide;

- The related and contentious issue of assisted suicide, with which politicians and citizens in more and more countries are grappling;

- Whether a taboo on taking one's life is helpful or harmful.

Most importantly, we will ponder whether or not suicide can really be prevented. We will see that predicting and preventing it is notoriously difficult. That does not stop well-meaning individuals and governments from doing something, on the principle that 'it's better to light one candle than to curse the dark'. People and politicians feel better when they are taking positive action of any description, even when they lack proof that it works.

We hope to address these issues systematically and to tease

out fact from fiction, pragmatism from hysteria and common sense from nonsense. We rely extensively on the research that has been carried out in this area and assess the evidence before arriving at conclusions. Readers will benefit from the views of a number of experts we interviewed.

This book should be of value to general-interest readers as well as those with a professional interest in the area. By the end, we hope readers will feel more informed and possess a greater appreciation of the breadth and depth of the topic. Compassion has a very important place in any discussion of suicide, but it must be associated with calm rationality. Only then will policy-makers, politicians and societies be able to deal with it in a sensible manner.

2.
Suicide: A Brief History

Uncovering historical evidence for the existence of suicide presents difficulties. Such deaths often have been concealed, but all indications are that suicide has existed in diverse societies in all eras. The first Western references to it – in a mix of historical, philosophical and literary sources – date from classical antiquity, between the seventh century BC and the fifth century AD.

In antiquity, the most celebrated case of suicide was that of Ajax. During the Greek war with Troy, Ajax was recognised as the main pretender to Achilles's position as the greatest Greek warrior. When Achilles was eventually killed, Ajax and his rival Odysseus ensured that Achilles's body was retrieved for burial. The pair then engaged in several days of competition to claim the prize of Achilles's armour and, with it, recognition as his rightful successor. Several days of close competition ensued. Odysseus eventually claimed victory and made a remarkable speech. Dejected and humiliated, Ajax saw no alternative but to end his life, which he did with his sword.

A number of examples of group suicides were reported in ancient times, which typically occurred because of military defeats. A mass suicide of 960 Jews is said to have taken place in 73 AD at the cliffs of Masada, which overlook the Dead Sea, during the first Jewish–Roman war. In order to avoid capture by the Romans and certain slaughter, each man killed his wife and children. The men then drew lots to determine which of them would kill each other. Only one actually killed himself, in the same way as Ajax – by falling on his sword.

Most sources from ancient Greece and Rome are very selective, concentrating on the suicides of aristocratic men. Women, slaves and those at the margins of society are all under-represented. Yet, in the figure of Lucretia, Rome provides a female suicide to rival that of Ajax. The daughter of a prominent Roman nobleman, Lucretia was raped by Sextus, the son of Rome's leader, Tarquin the Proud. Unable to cope with this dishonour, she revealed to her father what had happened, and then plunged a dagger in her own heart. This led to major political upheaval by encouraging the Romans to drive Tarquin and his family out of Rome in 508 BC, paving the way for the establishment of the first Roman republic.[1] Fascination with Lucretia's story would prompt Geoffrey Chaucer and William Shakespeare to pen poems about her centuries later. Titian and Rembrandt are just two of the many Renaissance artists who depicted her death in paintings.

The stories of Ajax's and Lucretia's suicides are known to us because of their aristocratic backgrounds. Based on the records of over 20,000 suicides from classical sources from a period spanning some 2,000 years, historian Anton van Hooff calculated a rate of suicide of 0.02 per 100,000 population per annum.[2] The modern Greek suicide rate, which is very low by international standards, was 3.8 per 100,000 in 2012. The 190-fold difference in these figures strongly suggests that many ancient suicides went unrecorded. This probably includes most suicides by people from non-aristocratic backgrounds. Van Hooff argues that it is usually because of extraordinary traits that we come to know about the suicides of those from other backgrounds. Unwavering loyalty is one such trait, so we know about the suicides of Cleopatra's two female slaves, Charmion and Eiras, who chose to die with her.[3]

The Christian taboo on suicide forms the backdrop for any examination of suicide in the Middle Ages. Suicide did not go away, but uncovering evidence of it became more difficult. People taking their own lives, and those closest to them, often made great efforts to conceal such deaths. A legal code from the French city of Lille in the thirteenth century urged suspicion of suicide when a dead body was found, even when the possibility of suicide was not reported, 'for he who attempts this desperate act never willingly does it openly'.[4]

In many European states, the property and assets of those who took their own lives were confiscated. After suicide was made illegal in England in the thirteenth century, those guilty of *felo de se* ('felon of himself' or suicide) forfeited their property to the king, although exceptions were occasionally made if it could be shown the person had been *non compos mentis* (of unsound mind). Because the monarchy was entitled to take possession of the goods of those who committed suicide, suicides began to be reported to the King's Bench in England and Wales. Records survive from 1485 until 1714 of cases reported, although these definitely do not include all suicides during that period.[5] In France too, until just before the Revolution of 1789, a self-killer's assets became the property of the king.

In the nineteenth century, technological advances led people to choose newer methods to end their own lives. The advent of the railway introduced the spectre of people throwing themselves in front of trains. Firearms and widely available poisons also become popular suicide methods. New theories and explanations for what drove people to suicide also emerged, and the first serious studies of suicide, including *Le Suicide* by Emile Durkheim, are from this period.

A rich history of suicide can also be uncovered outside of the West. The ancient sacred Indian texts, the Vedas, referred to suicide as far back as 4,000 BC. They permitted self-killing. Undoubtedly, the most infamous Indian tradition relating to suicide is *sati*. This custom involves a widow joining her dead husband on his funeral pyre. There are references to *sati* from the fourth century BC, but it did not grow in popularity until the twelfth century AD, when the practice spread among the Brahmins of Bengal. *Sati* was often not voluntary – many women were forced into it. The spread of *sati* at this time may have been linked to a law that introduced inheritance for widows.

The British imperial authorities eventually outlawed *sati* in 1829, and the persistence of the practice, despite the law, was cited as a justification for the continuation of British rule. *Sati* continued after Indian independence and occurred sporadically in certain parts of the country in the later twentieth century. The Indian state of Rajasthan introduced its Commission of Sati (Prevention) Act in 1987.

One of the earliest Japanese references to suicide is from the fourth century AD. It concerns the younger brother of the sixteenth emperor of Japan, Nintoku Tennō. Prior to assuming the throne, Nintoku is said to have disputed his own right to become emperor, insisting that his younger brother was more worthy. His younger brother, in turn, insisted that Nintoku should assume the throne. A comical interregnum continued for three years, as each brother sought to outdo the other in his show of modesty. This ended when the younger brother decided he would never be able to overcome Nintoku's determination. As he believed that the situation was placing the empire in danger, he took his own life.[6]

More recently, during the Second World War, there is the example of the Japanese *kamikaze* pilots. They sacrificed their lives for the empire by deliberately crashing their planes into Allied ships and are an example of *giseishi* or sacrificial suicide. During the Battle of Okinawa, which lasted from April to June of 1945, 4,000 Japanese planes were destroyed by the Allies, and 1,900 of these were *kamikaze* planes.[7] Alert to the existence of *kamikaze* pilots, ships with anti-aircraft guns usually destroyed their planes prior to the 'successful' completion of their missions.

This sacrificial form of suicide, in which enemies are also killed in support of political and military goals, has since then become more familiar to us via suicide attacks by Tamil separatists in Sri Lanka and Islamic fundamentalists in the Middle East and beyond.

Box 2.1 | The Word 'Suicide'

In spite of including thirteen suicides in his plays, William Shakespeare never actually used the word 'suicide'. It did not appear in the English language until Sir Thomas Browne's *Religio Medici* was published in 1642, although the Oxford English Dictionary dates its first usage to 1651. The German word *selbstmord* (self-murder) came into usage at roughly the same time. Both words signify sinful acts.

Ancient Greek and Roman descriptions of suicides did not have such negative connotations. The most commonly used ancient Greek word, *authocheir*, means to act with one's own hand. For anti-psychiatrist Thomas Szasz, the emergence of the noun 'suicide', to be distinguished from the verbs and verbal nouns that were used by the Greeks and Romans, indicated a dramatic shift, from viewing suicide as a self-determined act towards viewing it as a deed for which the person who kills himself may not be responsible.[8]

The English language has much less flexibility than other languages when it comes to describing suicide. English has no words, for instance, that allow speakers to identify forms of suicide that we might approve of. The Japanese word *jisatsu* implies a negative act, but other words – such as *jiketsu* and *jisai* – refer to an honourable act carried out in the public interest.

Attitudes and Reactions to Suicide

Signs surround suicide hotspots nowadays, urging those thinking of killing themselves to reconsider and to make contact with crisis services. This reflects the compassion now shown to those who see suicide as the best solution to life's problems and the obligation felt by society to prevent suicide. After an unsuccessful suicide attempt, care, kindness and help with overcoming the distress that sparked the suicidal impulse are typically offered. This has not always been the attitude towards suicide.

Although suicide has always been present, attitudes and reactions to it have by no means been constant. Medieval Western societies approved of severe punishments for suicide attempters and the grisly treatment of suicide fatalities; the mutilation of corpses was common. In ancient Greece and Rome on the other hand, suicide could sometimes be represented as a thing of beauty. Seneca, a Roman Stoic philosopher and statesman, reacting to the suicide of the incorruptible Roman politician and enemy of Caesar, Cato the Younger, said: 'Never could Jupiter have seen a fairer thing on earth than Cato's suicide.'[9] Seneca himself went on to die by suicide after being implicated in a plot to kill the emperor Nero.

Classical antiquity is the period in Western history when approval of and admiration for self-killing can be unearthed, which contrasts most starkly with medieval and modern attitudes. In ancient Greece, the suicides of Ajax and Lucretia illustrate what Anton van Hooff describes as a 'shame culture', in which heroes paid plenty of attention to how they were viewed by others.[10] Humiliated and dishonoured, both Ajax and Lucretia knew that suicide would gain them respect from their peers. Such was the seriousness with which suicide was viewed that ancient Athens even legislated for a form of assisted suicide. Permission to kill yourself, and the means to do it with poisonous hemlock, could be provided by the Athenian authorities if you successfully pleaded your case before the Senate.

Suicide did not *always* meet with the approval of the Greeks, however. Aristotle mentioned punishments imposed on those who had attempted suicide, including fines and losses of political rights. He and Plato considered suicide in a number of their works, and they both generally condemned it. Aristotle believed that a person who displayed courage in the face of death was noble, and so, by extension, suicide was the act of a coward. Because the law did not allow for suicide, it must be forbidden, Aristotle argued; the self-killer was acting in an unjust manner towards the state. Plato's objection to suicide centred on his view of man as belonging to the gods. During our lives, we act like guards on behalf of the gods and are not allowed to leave our posts whenever we see fit, he believed. In his *Phaedo* – which details the death of his teacher, Socrates, after consuming hemlock – Plato stated clearly that suicide was not lawful. In *Laws*, he outlined appropriate punishments. His ideal state would have punished self-inflicted death with burial 'ingloriously on the borders . . . in such places as are uncultivated and nameless', with 'no column or inscription'.[11] He allowed, however, that some suicides could be justified, making exceptions for those coping with extreme misfortune or intolerable shame.

Roman law recognised that many suicides were rational and therefore had to be legislated for. Reasons that might lead a man to kill himself rationally included pain or sickness, a fear of dishonour and *taedium vitae* (weariness of life), which was probably akin to what we now call depression. Among those not allowed to kill themselves were slaves and soldiers. This, of course, had nothing to do with any moral or religious disapproval of suicide and everything to do with the bottom line.[12] Slaves were the property of their masters and soldiers belonged to the state. Any societal approval of suicide that existed among the ancient Greeks and Romans would not survive the Christian prohibition on suicide, which was most strongly associated with Augustine of Hippo.

That the Christian church would come to regard suicide as an abominable sin was not inevitable. The Old Testament included not only the story of the heroic suicide of Samson, but also the stories of three other self-inflicted deaths – those of Saul, Abimelech and Achitophel – that were not condemned. Even the death of Jesus might be understood as a suicide, as the English poet John Donne insisted, when writing a controversial defence of voluntary death in the seventeenth century. The cult of martyrdom that

Christianity created among its early adherents, coupled with Christian doctrine on the joys of the afterlife, made death in defence of the faith an appealing prospect. The line between death by execution and an eager suicide was not always easily drawn, given the zeal for martyrdom that existed. All of this posed a challenge for early Church leaders like Augustine.

Augustine, however, was able to build upon some of the negative attitudes to suicide that existed in antiquity. Like Plato, he believed that our lives were not ours to take, having been granted as gifts from God. The man who ended his own life prematurely to avoid suffering or some earthly challenge was abandoning God's pre-ordained plan for him. What was novel about Augustine's view on suicide emerged from his analysis of the world through the prism of sin. For Augustine, the terrible sin of murder was prohibited by the biblical commandment 'Thou shalt not kill,' and this extended to killing oneself.

Augustine would be largely guided by the Gospels' messages on suicide. Matthew's account of Judas Iscariot's suicide was, therefore, crucial. Augustine charged Judas with committing two crimes: betraying Christ and killing himself. His suicide aggravated, rather than expiated, the guilt he felt for committing the first crime. The account of Jesus rejecting Satan's suggestion that he throw himself from the Temple also allowed Augustine to pronounce that suicide was the work of the Devil.

Where there is sin, someone must be guilty of that sin, and yet Augustine did not always locate that guilt in the most obvious of places. His novel analysis of the rape and subsequent suicide of the Roman heroine Lucretia led him to suggest that she had killed herself because of a guilty pleasure she felt while being raped.[13]

Augustine's pronouncements would later be refined by others, such as Thomas Aquinas, but his condemnations were the crucial foundation for the Christian prohibition of suicide as reflected in canon law. The Christian classification of suicide as an abominable sin was formalised at the Council of Arles in 452 AD, when suicide was officially condemned as a crime. Thereafter, the Church's position became more unforgiving. The Council of Braga of 562 decided to deny all suicides the right to be buried in consecrated ground. The Council of Toledo in 693 resolved to excommunicate those who survived suicide attempts.

Christianity profoundly shaped Western society during the Middle Ages. The church's views mattered and heavily influenced societal attitudes. Papal statements such as Pope Nicolas I's suggestion that 'the bodies of suicides might offend the nostrils of the living'[14] reflected the church's continued abhorrence of suicide throughout the period. They also gave licence to sanctions introduced by secular authorities, which reflected church and popular attitudes.

Alexander Murray's forensic analysis of legal instruments from the later medieval period, in the second book of his trilogy Suicide in the Middle Ages, identifies the variety of punishments that could be meted out to a self-killer even after his death.[15] Consider the mid-fourteenth-century 'Goslar statutes', which originated in the Prussian town after which they were named, but were adopted by many other towns and cities. They specified that when a suicide's body was removed from a dwelling, it should not be taken out through the main entrance but under the threshold or out the window. Murray speculates that this may have been because of a belief that this prevented a suicide's ghost from returning to the house.[16]

Defilement of corpses was routine. French and German sources indicate that bodies were often dragged by horses, and that corpses were sometimes further mutilated by hanging. In German regions, bodies were burned in fields or at road junctions, placed in barrels before being thrown into local rivers and even disposed of at local refuse pits. In 1288, the entire 'execution' of a man who had killed himself in Paris was repeated because, although his body had already been hung, the local abbey had neglected to drag it though the streets.[17]

Negative attitudes to suicide persisted into the early modern period of Western history, with some of the harsher penalties being introduced in the sixteenth century. The practice of driving a stake through the body of someone who had taken their own life emerged at this point in England and in parts of northern and eastern Germany. Yet, it is also at this time that a relaxation of the Christian taboo first emerged. They may still have largely condemned suicide, but significant religious figures such as Thomas More and Martin Luther were less hostile to it: More maintained that compassion should be shown towards those who suffer, and Luther insisted that a suicide's soul was not necessarily condemned for eternity. The idea that many people killed themselves because of madness became more widely accepted. Where this could be shown, Luther insisted that self-killers could not be held responsible for their actions and were therefore not guilty of sin.

It was not until the Enlightenment, from the late seventeenth century to the late eighteenth century, that there was a major shift away from viewing voluntary death as a sin. Some key Enlightenment figures such as Immanuel Kant continued to condemn suicide, but the Age of Reason challenged church orthodoxy and enabled philosophers like David Hume to put forward the explosive position that an individual had a right to suicide, based on the principle of autonomy. In his essay 'Of Suicide', Hume articulates a robust defence of rational suicide, insisting that old age, sickness or misfortune made suicide a sensible option for the person whose life was otherwise too burdensome to continue. He believed that 'no man ever threw away life, while it was worth keeping'.[18] So controversial was Hume's position that, despite being penned in 1755 and circulating clandestinely for years, it was not published until after his death in 1783.

It was during the eighteenth century that the first asylums for the care of the mentally ill opened. More compassion was shown towards those who engaged in suicidal behaviour. The old practices of defiling corpses eventually went out of use, and laws in many Western European countries began to change. Suicide was decriminalised in France in 1810. In 1823, a change to the burial laws in England prohibited the burial of suicides' corpses at crossroads and outlawed the driving of stakes through corpses' hearts. Even those found guilty of *felo de se* in England were entitled to be buried in churchyards, although, in practice, many were buried at the backs of churches.[19]

As more reliable data became available in the nineteenth century, accurate calculations of the prevalence of suicide could be carried out. These confirmed that suicide rates in Western countries increased during that century. While an apparent increase in the sixteenth century had led to harsher penalties, this nineteenth-century increase prompted efforts to understand suicide, using new approaches. Emile Durkheim published his hugely influential *Le Suicide* in 1897, in which he maintained that people do not kill themselves because of private circumstances such as mental illness, but rather because of social forces.

The development of more-tolerant attitudes, however, did not mean that centuries-old stigmas disappeared overnight. Some punishments persisted into the twentieth century. A court on the Isle of Man ordered a teenager who had attempted suicide in 1969 to be whipped. Suicide was decriminalised in England and Wales in 1961, however. Ireland followed suit in 1993.

★

In contrast to Western societies, Japanese society, throughout its history, has largely approved of suicide and accepted it as a legitimate response to shameful circumstances. Suicide has never been prohibited by law in Japan. Attitudes there have been heavily influenced by Shintoism and Buddhism; in Japan, one can be both Shinto and Buddhist. Japanese Buddhist traditions have portrayed life on earth as full of suffering and idealised an escape from the misery of this 'monstrous' world. Kichinosuke Tatai argues that, as a consequence, Japanese minds have been preoccupied with death, how we die and life after death.[20] Shintoism emphasises respect for tradition and loyalty to the empire and the fatherland, which must take precedence over loyalty to ourselves and our families.

Harakiri or *seppuku*, which mean 'belly cutting', first emerged in the twelfth century AD, and numerous accounts survive of soldiers and samurai killing themselves in this way. It was intended as a means for samurai to prevent their capture by an enemy, or as a noble way out if they had committed serious crimes or otherwise brought shame on themselves. It was universally regarded as an honourable and courageous way to die. When the friends of Julius Caesar's enemy, Cato the Younger, found him close to death after he had stabbed himself, they did their best to keep him alive; a friend or relative of a Japanese samurai about to take his own life was, instead, likely to assist him and show approval by perhaps beheading the samurai once he had already sliced open his own belly.

Japanese troops in the Second World War were expected to follow the *bushido* or code of the samurai. The code, however, exerted influence beyond military personnel. A number of Japanese government ministers killed themselves following Japan's defeat. Thousands of ordinary Japanese also took their own lives, out of a sense of personal shame over the defeat.

Historical Suicide Prevention

Efforts to prevent people from killing themselves are as old as suicide itself. After the death of one of Pythagoras's pupils, apparently due to the humiliation of a public rebuke by the great Greek mathematician, Pythagoras resolved to censure his students in private.[21]

The Greek historian Plutarch described a wave of suicides among the young women of the Greek city of Miletus. The elders of the city were at a loss as to how to prevent so many women from hanging themselves. The tears of parents, the comforting words of friends and attempts to watch over the women proved ineffective. Eventually, someone stumbled on the idea that publicly displaying the naked corpses of women who committed suicide might be a deterrent. And so it was. Vanity and fear of what would be done to their bodies after death worked where all other efforts had failed. The spate of suicides suddenly came to an end.

Before the nineteenth century, however, efforts to stop people from killing themselves were isolated and tended to occur following multiple suicides. So it was with the response to the thousands of suicides that resulted from the barbaric treatment of the indigenous population during the Spanish conquest of the West Indies and the Americas. In the sixteenth century, many people there took their own lives rather than submit to vicious slavery or annihilation by the Spanish. Faced with a labour shortage in Haiti, the Spanish convinced people there that, if they did not stop taking their own lives, the colonists would also end their own lives – and pursue them into the afterlife, where they would mete out even harsher punishments.[22]

The Christian taboo on suicide, reflected in hostile attitudes and ecclesiastical and state sanctions, served as the main preventative measure prior to the Enlightenment. Although, on occasion, radical religious beliefs such as the Calvinist doctrine of predestination may have caused people who were convinced they were damned to end their lives, harsh Christian attitudes almost certainly reduced deaths from suicide. By how much? It is not possible to quantify how successful such sanctions were, but there was a belief in the eighteenth and nineteenth centuries that the spread of Enlightenment ideas that challenged traditional orthodoxies, and the relaxation of hostile attitudes, were leading to more self-inflicted deaths. What undoubtedly would not have been possible if attitudes had not softened was the emergence of the first systematic efforts to prevent suicide.

In her history, *Suicide in Victorian and Edwardian England*, Olive Anderson describes how the nineteenth and early twentieth centuries witnessed the growing medicalisation of suicide prevention, the development of more compassionate services for those who survived suicide attempts, the birth of the suicide-prevention agency and the restriction of access to the means of suicide.[23] All of these techniques are still in use today.

Anderson shows how, paradoxically, a new offence of attempted suicide created in England and Wales in 1845 actually helped to foster more compassionate practices. Rather than punish or jail those who tried to end their lives, magistrates who heard cases of attempted suicide were likely to refer people to a variety of organisations that offered their services to the prisons and the courts. People might be sent away to reformatories to deal with alcohol problems, or even offered a seaside holiday.

This new, more compassionate approach fostered a climate in which it was possible for the London Anti-Suicide Bureau to open its doors in 1901. This was the world's first organisation specifically dedicated to preventing suicide. It departed radically from previous prevention strategies. Because it invited anyone with suicidal thoughts to contact it, the Bureau was able to assist people from a much broader section of society. It was not only those who had already tried to kill themselves who availed of its services.

The drug and alcohol problems linked to many suicide attempts in the nineteenth century did not disappear, but some of the reasons that people contacted the Bureau were new. Financial difficulties prompted many desperate people to make contact, so the Bureau offered practical help – clothing and perhaps a little money – and tried to bring about reconciliations with friends and family members. It also negotiated with creditors.[24]

The Bureau's most important legacy is that its model of suicide prevention still survives today, in the form of suicide-prevention organisations and crisis services, such as the Samaritans, which operate in the United Kingdom and Ireland. The belief that suicide is best prevented by convincing people in crisis to seek help also remains central to modern suicide-prevention efforts.

The Bureau's model for suicide prevention had its detractors. Dr E. F. Talbot McCarthy, a visiting physician to the British Hospital and formerly 'visitor in lunacy' of the High Court of Justice in Ireland, suggested that most suicidal impulses were very sudden and, as such, the Bureau would only be able to proffer assistance to a small minority of the people who needed it.[25]

If, as Dr McCarthy suggested, many suicides were impulsive, then organisations such as the Bureau would not be sufficient to stop self-killing. Other strategies were needed to target people who, while in the midst of an acute suicidal crisis, were unlikely to think of getting help from an organisation. Making it more difficult for people to physically access the methods used to end lives had an important role to play. Anti-suicide structures were constructed amid public fears of copycat deaths at suicide hotspots. For example, an iron cage was built in 1842 around the gallery of the Monument to the Great Fire of London after a number of people leapt to their deaths from there.

Changes to the law sought to restrict access to suicide methods – especially drugs and poisons, which had grown in popularity. The Pharmacy Act of 1868 set up a schedule of poisons that could be sold only by registered pharmacists. More were added as their dangers became apparent. In this way, carbolic acid, a disinfectant used by women to kill themselves, was added in 1900.

The eighteenth century gave birth to the 'lunatic' asylum and, by the following century, this was seen as the panacea for all problems associated with mental illness, including suicide. The seventh Earl of Shaftesbury, a prominent social reformer, told the British House of Lords in 1882 that the best means of preventing suicide was early treatment and care in an asylum. This belief became accepted wisdom, and general practitioners in the late nineteenth century who identified any dangerous symptoms of depression preferred to send their patients to such institutions.

Notwithstanding Britain's recognition of the merits of other approaches, confinement to an asylum became the dominant means relied upon to prevent suicide. So there was considerable pressure on those working in asylums to prevent deaths. Anderson reports that, in 1911, only 0.14 percent of all deaths in English and Welsh county and borough asylums were suicides,[26] so those who were admitted had very little chance of killing themselves.

Suicides, though, were prevented at great cost to the patients. Mechanical restraints, including straitjackets, were regularly used. Many patients were placed in special wards, where they were under constant observation. Strict vigilance was the norm. Modern inpatient facilities may not be as restrictive as the Victorian asylums, but the public's belief that hospitalising people experiencing suicidal crises is the best way to prevent suicide persists.

★

Suicide, then, has always been of interest to those in positions of civil and religious leadership. Today, it is predominantly viewed as an unwise action, a permanent solution to temporary problems, a tragedy that devastates those left behind. This reflects modern values, the ways we have been socialised to view death and the ways we have been encouraged to assess the choice to exit life voluntarily.

The assumptions that we hold regarding suicide should, at a minimum, be questioned. Broadening our awareness of alternative historical views allows us to consider whether seemingly radical perspectives such as the Romans' acceptance of the legitimacy of rational suicide are actually sensible, when it comes to a small minority of cases.

In spite of the suffering it heaps upon families, the Christian attitude of hostility to suicide may provide some insight into how we might reduce its incidence. Punishing people who attempt suicide obviously has no place nowadays; compassion is clearly a more appropriate response. Yet, we should discourage suicide, in the vast majority of cases, and maintaining a taboo around such behaviour – while not stigmatising distressed individuals – may make it less appealing to desperate people. This remains the central conflict: compassion, understanding and the condoning of suicide, with the possibility of increased incidence, versus stigma and disapproval, with the possibility of prevention.

However, what those who treat distressed people, friends and family members of victims, and all of us with an interest in self-inflicted death must acknowledge is that, as suicide has always existed, it is inevitable that it will continue.

3.
Answering Key
Suicide Questions:
Why? What?

After a person takes their own life, loved ones, health professionals, communities and even the media try to retrace that person's
thoughts and steps, to understand more about their death. They
usually ask why the person did it. Knowledge about suicide has
advanced significantly over the years, which means we can provide some partial answers. Work by clinicians and suicide
researchers, as well as international data-collection efforts, also
allows us to understand how the impact of suicide differs across
the globe; some cultures and groups are more at risk than others.

Emile Durkheim's nineteenth-century definition highlighted
the key characteristics of such a death as being an act of the
deceased person himself, where lethal self-intent was present. It
remains as useful today to clarify what it is we are talking about
when we refer to suicide. Other aspects of 'what' – defining and
classifying suicide and other forms of suicidal behaviour – are
examined later in the chapter. Initially, we will focus on the question most people struggle with when someone they know takes
their own life.

Why?

That someone would really want to end his or her own life perplexes many of us. Life is usually seen by the religious and the secular alike as a precious gift, which a person should hold onto. Explaining why someone has died by suicide is not straightforward. Usually, there will be multiple reasons or factors that lead to such a decision, with suicide the end result of interactions among multiple vulnerabilities. Such vulnerabilities can also be understood as risk factors and a large number can be identified that make it much more likely for certain people to kill themselves than the rest of the population.

Male gender is strongly associated with self-inflicted death, especially in developed countries where, typically, men are between two and four times more likely than women to kill themselves. Hopelessness and personality traits such as impulsivity and aggressiveness make some people more prone to suicidal behaviour. Alcohol and drug abuse increase risk for individuals both in the short term, following intoxication or withdrawal, and in the long term, due to the ill effects of substance abuse over a sustained period. The World Health Organization has stated that more than one-fifth (22 percent) of global suicides would not occur if alcohol were not consumed.[1] It is also estimated that 30 to 40 percent of those who die by suicide have some significant physical illness. Suicide rates are especially high among people with terminal illnesses, including cancer and HIV/AIDS.

Risk increases for those who have undergone traumatic experiences, particularly in early life, such as childhood physical or sexual abuse. People who are unemployed also have higher rates. A previous suicide attempt is one of the strongest known predictors of subsequent suicide, as between 7 and 12 percent of those who make a suicide attempt will have ended their lives within ten years. We will now look at three of the most significant risk factors in more detail: mental illness, family history of suicide and social isolation.

Mental Illness

Ever since the medicalisation of suicide facilitated challenging the view of it as a sinful deed, suicide in the public imagination has been synonymous with mental illness. It is now well established that a diagnosis of mental illness elevates risk significantly. As many as one in every eight people with a diagnosis of schizophrenia will eventually end up killing themselves, and there are also high rates of suicide among those with depression and borderline personality disorder. This does not mean that all suicides are linked to mental illness; people choose voluntary death in the absence of mental illness, and independently of it. There is, for example, the impulsive suicide carried out over some relatively minor mishap, often under the influence of alcohol. And terminally ill people who choose to end their lives prematurely are usually not mentally ill.

Studies called psychological autopsies are largely responsible for establishing such a strong link between suicide and mental illness. They try to replicate forensic autopsies in order to establish why someone killed themself. Rather than carrying out a physical examination of the deceased person, however, they involve collecting information from multiple sources, such as interviews with family members and close friends of the deceased. Typically, they find that more than 90 percent of suicides are associated with mental illness.

Though psychological autopsies provide valuable information

about the lives of those who have died, there are problems with the methods used to link fatalities with mental illness. Doubts exist over the instruments that have been used to retrospectively diagnose the deceased. Interviews with people close to those who have died also create a real risk that mental illness will be incorrectly attributed to the dead person. It can serve as a suitable explanation for many suicides that otherwise lack obvious causes. Though a different cultural context applies, more recent studies from Asia suggest that only about half of suicides are associated with mental illness.[2] Complicating the discussion further is the fact that the terms 'mental illness' and 'mental health' mean different things to different people.

Many experts, such as Professor Ella Arensman, director of research at the National Suicide Research Foundation in Ireland, caution against downplaying the link between mental illness and suicide. Arensman believes that someone who does not have a diagnosed mental illness but who, nevertheless, kills himself without speaking to others about the stresses and problems in his life is still clearly demonstrating an emotional vulnerability. She insists that such a vulnerability means that we cannot make a definitive, black-and-white assessment that there is no mental illness component to this person's suicide.[3] An opposing view put forward by the Australian psychiatrist Saxby Pridmore criticises the medicalisation of suicide and insists that the distress which precedes a suicide frequently arises from social and environmental stressors, not mental illness.

Family History

In 2009, almost half a century after the celebrated poet and novelist Sylvia Plath ended her life, her son, Nicholas Hughes, hung himself. If a parent engages in suicidal behaviour, his or her children are six times more likely than the general population to carry out a suicidal act. Losing a close family member to suicide heightens risk in a number of different ways. Hughes, like his famous mother, had experienced depression. We know that there is a genetic component to mental illness. This makes it more likely for people to develop certain mental illnesses, including depression and schizophrenia, and, therefore, indirectly transmits a risk of suicide. Some of the risk for suicide that is inherited is, nevertheless, likely to be independent of an association between our genes and mental illness.[4] Traits such as aggression and impulsivity also run in families.

Genes do not tell the whole story. When a family member ends his life, it may also lead to a culture of permission within that family. If my father's 'solution' to his difficulties was suicide, then I might think it appropriate for me to adopt the same 'solution' when I encounter life's inevitable setbacks. I may also just be imitating a behaviour that I had not been aware of before. If I revered the deceased family member, this type of copycat behaviour is more likely. Dysfunctional family environments, in which physical or sexual abuse or drug and alcohol abuse are routine, which played a role in a relative's suicide, will often remain dysfunctional after such a death. The exposure of other family members to further traumas means that they are at increased risk of ending their lives.

Social Isolation and Relationships

Rene Duignan is an Irish economist who has dedicated himself to fighting suicide in Japan, where he lives and works. He has drawn attention to the Japanese phenomenon of *hikikomori*, a disorder whereby people suffer from acute social withdrawal:

they may never leave their homes. There are hundreds of thousands of Japanese with the disorder, which contributes significantly to the 30,000 annual suicides in Japan. Duignan contends that the influence of Japanese technology – and of the computer-gaming industry, in particular – creates an image of a trendy country and promotes the apparent benefits of people getting lost in computer games. He maintains, however, that the reality of a society obsessed with technology can be much bleaker, allowing many Japanese people to function without ever leaving their apartments.[5] The power of the Internet means that everything from computer games to food and life's basic necessities can be ordered online.

Acute social isolation typifies the lives of many who kill themselves. A long period of loneliness in the year prior to suicide was reported for 46 percent of a sample of 190 suicides that occurred in Cork between 2008 and 2011, for example.[6] The American psychiatrist Jerome Motto has described a suicide note that deeply affected him and revealed the extent of one man's disconnectedness from society. He jumped from the Golden Gate Bridge after leaving behind a note that said, 'I'm going to walk to the bridge. If one person smiles at me on the way, I will not jump.'[7]

Towards a More Complete Understanding of Why

As well as individual vulnerabilities, there are societal and cultural traits that increase risk. Some cultures are more accepting of suicide, as is the case in Japan, which has a rich history of suicide and has always had elevated rates. Unemployment increases risk for individuals, but economic decline can also increase rates in a country as whole and make it more likely for people who retain their jobs to end their lives. We will explore this phenomenon in more detail later.

In most cases of voluntary death, the likelihood is that a myriad of risk factors and stressors were impinging upon individuals at the time of death. There is also likely to be significant overlap among many of these factors. So we know that childhood abuse may lead to the development of mental illness, which, in turn, is associated with poor physical health and personality traits such as oversensitivity and aggressiveness. This combination can be deadly when levels of distress reach such a point that suicide is seen as the only solution.

At the same time, we must not make the mistake of assuming that suicide is an inevitable outcome for anyone with multiple vulnerabilities. Someone with psychosis who experiences interpersonal difficulties and has to cope with the suicide of a sibling will undoubtedly lead a life full of challenges, but he may never contemplate making an attempt on his life. He may possess some of the long list of factors that protect against suicide, including resilience, adaptability and cultural and religious beliefs that oppose suicide.

Box 3.1 | Does Religion Protect People Against Suicide?

Thankfully, religiously sanctioned punishments meted out to suicide attempters and the families of suicide victims are largely relics of the past. Even though compassionate attitudes and practices are now approved of by many religious leaders, the three main Abrahamic religions – Christianity, Islam and Judaism – continue to oppose suicidal acts. In November 2014, a senior Vatican official described the assisted suicide of a twenty-nine-year-old American woman who had inoperable brain cancer as 'reprehensible'.[8] The official clarified that he was not passing judgement against the woman herself, but wished to point out that 'the gesture in and of itself should be condemned'.[9]

Islam has certainly been more resistant to sanctioning compassionate attitudes than Christianity and Judaism. Sharia law guides the legal systems in ten countries, for example, and provides for sanctions against those who try to kill themselves. In practice, people are rarely prosecuted. Most Muslim countries, particularly in the Arab world, record very low rates of suicide. Many pious Muslims in acute distress are likely choosing to reject suicide because of Islam's condemnatory views.

A Catholic expert on religious education, Fr Gerard Conlon, linked the absence of religion in young Irish people's lives to an increase in suicidal behaviours among them. He lamented the fact that little reference is made to religion as a means of reducing the prevalence of suicide.[10] Can religion offer real protection against suicidal behaviour? Robust research data from the US shows that people who regularly attend religious services are much less likely to end their own lives than others.[11] After accounting for all other factors, the study found that someone who attended services at least twenty-four times a year was 67 percent less likely to die by suicide than a person who went less often. Some of this decrease in risk can likely be attributed to the sense of belonging people derive from religion. Theological opposition to suicide doubtless also plays a role.

The presence of meaningful relationships in our lives protects against social isolation and suicide. Durkheim's observation that married people are less likely to kill themselves has been confirmed in more-recent analyses, although the protective effect is much stronger for men. Consider the findings of Ireland-based researchers Paul Corcoran and Aaron Nager, who looked at suicide trends in Northern Ireland between 1996 and 2005.[12] They found that no matter what your age, if you were a man who had never married, your risk automatically went up. Among women though, only young single women were at increased risk.

While marriage offers protection against suicidal behaviour, divorce increases risk. The same Northern Irish data showed that among people over the age of fifty-five, divorce made it three times more likely that men and women would kill themselves. Widowhood, on the other hand, only increased risk for men.

The first comprehensive theory of suicide was offered in the nineteenth century by Emile Durkheim, whose interest in the issue was piqued following the suicide of one of his classmates and the apparent rise in European suicide rates at the time. Durkheim linked such increases to modernity and the associated weakening of family and community bonds, and he relied on suicide statistics in order to support his views.

The prevailing view then, as now, linked suicide almost exclusively with mental illness. Durkheim countered that this was hopelessly inadequate and completely ignored potent social forces. If mental illness was the primary reason people killed themselves, there should not be an enduring pattern of suicide rates differing dramatically between countries, he insisted. The prevalence of mental illness did not vary enough between countries to account for these differences. Among other observations he made that cast doubt on the medical model of suicide was that women had higher rates of mental illness but lower rates of suicide.

Durkheim's conclusions that marriage and parenthood protect against suicide, that people are less likely to kill themselves during wars than peacetime and that educated people are more likely to end their lives than those with less education have been confirmed by modern evidence. When he examined suicide rates in different parts of Switzerland, he found higher rates in the mainly Protestant cantons compared to the predominantly Catholic cantons. He assumed this would hold true elsewhere and attributed the lower suicide rate among Catholics to their higher degree of social integration, though there is no clear-cut evidence that this is actually the case today.

A recent contribution from Pridmore attempts to reconcile Durkheim's sociological perspective with the dominant medical model. Pridmore's clinical experience has left him very much aware of the contribution of mental illness to suicidal behaviour. Still, he concludes that the link is overestimated, primarily because of the incorrect medicalisation of human distress. Like many others, Pridmore recognises that voluntary death is rarely the result of a single event or stressor. It is, in his view, ultimately an escape strategy used by people who find themselves in a predicament, which he defines as 'a situation, especially an unpleasant, troublesome, or trying one, from which extraction is difficult'.[13] It is not necessarily death that they are seeking. Rather, death is the means by which people in crisis flee unbearable distress.

Two main types of predicament are identified. In the first, a mental illness is present and largely explains the suicide. In the second, mental illness is absent and social and environmental stressors are largely responsible for the distress that precedes the suicide. Pridmore's framework recognises that these two types of predicament frequently coexist just as multiple risk factors can interact to produce the distress that leads to a suicide. Ernest

Hemingway's suicide, which we will examine later, is seen, then, as the result of a predicament that was principally associated with mental illness, although his many vulnerabilities also included the abuse of alcohol, the loss of family members to suicide and chaotic interpersonal relationships.

Pridmore's 'suicide predicament' model describes a suicide-risk ladder that ascends from zero risk until it reaches a threshold of ten, at which suicide occurs. This model assumes that we all have a baseline tendency to suicide. This varies from person to person, however, and is subject to many influences. These include personality, early life experiences, culture, gender and past mental health. This baseline tendency is conceptualised as unlikely to shift dramatically during an individual's lifetime. 'Momentary position', as he terms it, is the suicide risk of any individual at a particular point in time. When predicaments arise, they can trigger strong suicidal impulses and pull this position towards the threshold at which suicide occurs. The impact of different stressors is highly relevant. Alcohol and drug intoxication, certain personality traits and the nature of stressors can all increase the acuity of a person's distress and propel them towards suicide.

The model acknowledges that the same predicament experienced by different people can produce very different outcomes. A troubled life marred by childhood abuse and neglect, personality traits such as aggressiveness, and a family history of suicide may leave a person with a high baseline tendency to suicide. A distressing experience, such as the ending of a significant relationship, may contribute to placing that person in a predicament that they seek to escape through death. Without such a troubled life, the person would have had a lower baseline, and probably possessed a number of protective factors (which are not shown in the model), so the suicide would have been unlikely to occur.

Figure 3.1 | Pridmore's Suicide Predicament Model

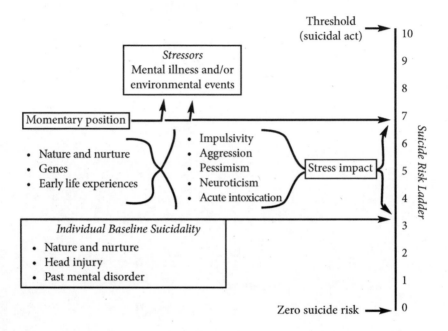

Source: Pridmore, S. *Suicide and Predicament: Life Is a Predicament.* Bentham Science Publishers, 2010.

Because Pridmore's model omits the many factors that protect against suicide, it does not adequately reflect why suicide happens so rarely. Still, it has a number of strengths, including the fact that it challenges the dominant medical model while integrating sociological approaches. Durkheim correctly identified the central role that social forces play in suicidal behaviour, but he shifted the focus too far away from mental illness and private and biological factors, which cannot be ignored. Pridmore recognises the multiple factors that contribute to suicide risk, often through strong interactions.

All of this is consistent with the results of research on why people seek to escape life. And yet, we must emphasise that we are trying to understand what is going on inside human brains – and it is difficult to think of a more complex structure. So there probably will always be uncertainty surrounding the reasons why people decide to end it all.

What? Defining and Classifying Suicide and Suicidal Behaviour

To arrive at a verdict of suicide in a coroner's hearing in Ireland today, the only additional requirement, beyond those set out in Durkheim's definition, is that the intentional lethal act that resulted in the person's death be proven beyond a reasonable doubt to have been self-inflicted.

Aside from these basic commonalities that all suicides share, are we always referring to the same thing when we talk about suicide? Far from it. Voluntary death should never be viewed as a unitary phenomenon. The death of the suicide bomber who blows themself up in the midst of a crowd of innocent bystanders is a world away from the self-inflicted death of someone debilitated by the pain brought on by terminal cancer. A useful way to categorise suicides would clearly assist us. Durkheim attempted to provide one, identifying four types of suicide, based on levels of integration and regulation in society.

Figure 3.2 | Durkheim's Typology of Suicide

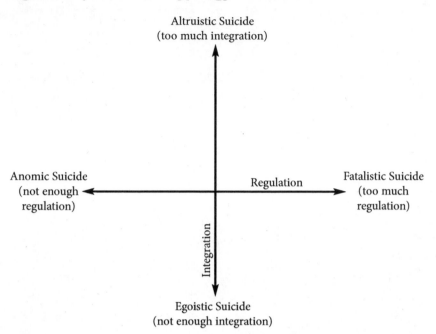

Source: Pope, W. *Durkheim's Suicide: A Classic Analysed*. Chicago: University of Chicago Press, 1976.

First, there are types of suicide characterised by too much and too little integration. Durkheim's 'egoistic suicide' can occur when a self-centred person's excessive individualism cuts him off from society. Durkheim believed that the higher suicide rates he observed in Protestant populations were explained by their lower levels of social integration, compared to Catholics and Jews. In contrast, what he labelled as 'altruistic suicide' is carried out by someone who, lacking an individualistic streak, believes his death is in the interest of others, as with the Japanese *kamikaze* pilots in the Second World War.

Durkheim also envisaged suicides as occurring when people experience too much or too little regulation in their lives. Prisoners or slaves likely experience too much control and may react by carrying out a 'fatalistic suicide'. The normal restraints of society could also abruptly change, such as during economic booms and busts. When a person's previous expectations and demands, which have developed during good economic times, can no longer be met, a form of alienation can develop, which Durkheim termed *anomie*, from the Greek word for 'without law'. 'Anomic suicide' can ensue. An economic boom can also unleash insatiable demands for material goods and frustration at an inability to obtain such goods could also lead to anomie. Combinations of Durkheim's types of suicide could also exist.

Ultimately, there are a vast number of ways in which self-inflicted death can be categorised, and the complexity of the phenomenon means that each is imperfect. The difficulty with Durkheim's classification system is the same as the difficulty with his theory of suicide: he does not allocate any role to mental illness. We know that there are suicides linked to mental illness and suicides that are not. There are also rational and irrational suicides, individual and group suicides and impulsive and non-impulsive suicides. Each type has its own particular nuances and characteristics. The strength of Durkheim's approach lies in his drawing attention to the social roots of many of these fatalities.

★

Suicide needs to be distinguished from two related non-lethal forms of suicidal behaviour. Suicidal ideation and suicide attempts are risk factors for suicide, but they occur far more frequently. Clearly, no suicide can occur without suicidal thoughts or ideas. Most psychiatrists would say that suicidal ideas are extremely common and, in most cases, fleeting. They often occur in the context of an emotional or life setback. These ideas are frequently expressed as part of everyday language, such as, 'If he doesn't agree to go out with me, I'll kill myself.' For the most part, they are not associated with any real threat. Even individuals who have suicidal ideas on a less-than-fleeting basis generally do not form any specific intentions to kill themselves, or develop specific plans or take steps to implement those plans.

Add actual suicidal intent into the mix, however, and suicidal ideation will often lead to a suicide attempt, which is distinguished from actual suicide because of its non-fatal outcome. Deliberate self-harm is yet another type of suicidal behaviour. It can involve behaviours such as cutting or burning. There is clear intent to injure, but lethal intent is typically absent. Using a variety of data sources, we will look more closely at how common suicidal ideation, self-harm resulting in hospital treatment and actual suicide are in Ireland.

Along with six colleagues, Irish psychiatrist Patricia Casey examined the extent of suicidal ideation in Ireland and four other European countries in a 2008 study, by assessing responses to items on a well-known measure of depression known as the Beck Depression Inventory.[14] They found that suicidal ideation was reported by a relatively large percentage of Irish people. Between 12.8 percent (urban males) and 19.8 percent (urban females) of Irish respondents indicated that they had suicidal ideas, which was higher than in any of the other countries examined. For example, between 1.1 and 3.4 percent of Spanish respondents to the survey indicated that they had experienced suicidal thoughts or ideas. Some of this variation may have been due to methodology (self-reports are unreliable) and cross-cultural differences in interpretations of the questions asked. Still, the differences are striking.

So a relatively high proportion of Irish people form ideas about killing themselves. Yet, only 0.2 percent of Irish people engage in self-harming behaviours that require hospital treatment.[15] (Irish data does not distinguish between deliberate self-harm and suicide attempts.) Of course, we need to account for those who self-harm and are not treated in hospitals. Even if we assume that, say, twice as many people who self-harm do not end up in hospitals, that would mean that 0.6 percent of Irish people self-harm, a substantially smaller proportion than that which has suicidal thoughts.

Table 3.1 | Prevalence of Suicidal Ideation and Suicidal Behaviours

Category of Suicidal Ideation/Behaviour	Male Prevalence	Female Prevalence
Suicidal ideation	12.8 to 15 percent of Irish men in 2008	14.1 to 19.8 percent of Irish women in 2008
Self-harm resulting in hospital treatment	0.2 percent of Irish men in 2012	0.2 percent of Irish women in 2012
Completed suicide	0.017 percent of Irish men in 2012	0.005 percent of Irish women in 2012

Sources: Casey, P., Dunn, G., Kelly, B. D., Lehtinen, V., Dalgard, O. S., Dowrick, C. et al. 'The Prevalence of Suicidal Ideation in the General Population: Results from the Outcome of Depression International Network (ODIN) Study'. In *Social Psychiatry and Psychiatric Epidemiology*. 2008; 43: pp299-304. National Suicide Research Foundation. 'National Registry of Deliberate Self-Harm Ireland Annual Report 2013'. Cork: NSRF, 2013. WHO. 'Preventing Suicide: A Global Imperative – Annex 1'. Geneva: WHO, 2014.

Suicide itself is rarer than either suicidal ideation or self-harm requiring hospitalisation. Approximately 500 people out of Ireland's 4.5 million kill themselves each year. In 2012, there were 16.9 male suicide fatalities and 5.2 female suicide deaths for every 100,000 Irish people. Five hundred deaths a year strikes many people as a large figure, and the Irish media certainly conveys the impression that there are a disproportionately large number of suicide victims in the country. Looking at the figures objectively, though, shows that suicide is a very rare event and that there is actually a very low likelihood of anyone who has suicidal thoughts going on to kill themself. The vast majority of people who self-harm or attempt suicide will also never go on to end their lives.

To complicate matters somewhat, a previous suicide attempt remains the strongest risk factor for a subsequent suicide. At the same time, only around 40 percent of those who die by their own hand have previously made an attempt. So, even if we rely on the strongest predictor of suicide, we will fail to identify most of those who will eventually die in this way.

These complex relationships between different types of suicidal behaviour and the relative frequency of suicidal ideation compared to actual suicide creates particular difficulties for mental-health professionals who must treat people in crisis. Among the multitude of patients who present with suicidal thoughts and ideas, they are expected to assess suicide risk and ultimately predict who is in imminent danger.

Box 3.2 | Predicting Suicide

Most psychiatrists probably concur with the recent assessment made on behalf of Ireland's largest psychiatric hospital, St Patrick's, that 'mental-health professionals are not able to predict suicide and there is no test or clinical assessment which is either valid or reliable in this area'.[16] All the same, it is difficult to find too many psychiatrists who do not assess for suicide risk, not least because of the fear that they may face a claim for negligence in the aftermath of a suicide fatality. If there were an assessment that could be relied upon, it would need to be both sensitive, correctly predicting suicide when it should (few false positives), and specific, correctly predicting that someone will not take his own life (few false negatives). In reality, every single suicide assessment throws up large numbers of false positives and false negatives.

This seems at odds with the fact that we can identify a large number of risk factors for suicide. Some, such as mental illness or a previous suicide attempt, create substantially elevated risk among people, compared to the general population. But the fact remains that these risk factors are still very common and are shared by large numbers of people who will never attempt to kill themselves. We noted earlier that one in eight people with schizophrenia (about 12 percent) will end up killing themselves, compared to 1.5 percent of the general population. What this also means, of course, is that the vast majority of people with a schizophrenia diagnosis (88 percent) will not die by suicide. The same applies to most people with suicidal thoughts and ideas and most people who have previously made an attempt on their life.

The reasons for a suicide are, as we have seen, complex and usually multifactorial. Crucially, suicide remains a rare event and trying to predict any rare event, in the absence of valid and reliable information, is almost an impossible task.

Assessing and predicting suicide is not routinely carried out with a focus on lifetime risk. Over a short timescale, trying to predict who will die is even more challenging. The chance of a patient with schizophrenia dying from suicide over the course of one year is less than one in one hundred, and the chance of that patient dying over the course of one month is less than one in one thousand.

Although the likelihood of anyone dying by suicide in the short term is very low, because it is unpredictable, many doctors take the default option of hospitalising – often inappropriately – patients who present with suicidal ideation.

These are the challenges associated with predicting suicide amongst patients who seek help and are labelled 'high-risk'. But most people who end their lives do not seek help from health services or crisis services because of mental illness or other stressors. Often, family members will note that a suicide came as a complete shock. How can we then predict which 500 Irish people will kill themselves in a given year?

When someone dies by suicide, it may appear clear in hindsight that they were struggling with severe suicidal ideation and preparing for death – but this is muddled thinking. We would have to put ourselves in that position in advance and see if we could have predicted the death and then perhaps have done something differently, which may have been effective. Establishing the reasons why someone killed themself is another formidable challenge. With the person best-placed to provide the answer no longer present, a complete answer will rarely ever be realised for an individual.

Mental illness is an important factor behind many suicides, but it is by no means associated with as many as we are led to believe. There will usually be many overlapping reasons why such deaths take place. Part of the success of the human enterprise has been the evolved ability to develop in response to stress, allied to self-preservation. Stress can become unbearable for some people, though, who seek to escape and ultimately overwhelm their instinct for self-preservation.

4.
Answering Other Key Suicide Questions

Emile Durkheim's interest in suicide was stirred by the variation in rates he observed among different countries and regions, and the persistence of these differences from one year to the next. Reliable evidence confirms that the impact of suicide across the world today is incredibly uneven. The ways in which people in crisis choose to end their lives also vary around the world. Age and gender both influence how likely we are to end our lives.

This chapter presents a contemporary global overview of suicide by providing answers to some of the remaining questions that surround self-inflicted death. How many people kill themselves in different countries? How do they exit life? Who is at greatest risk? This chapter comes with a 'data health warning'. Readers are advised that we present lots of data in order to try and answer these questions.

How Many? Where? | A Global Overview of Suicide Rates

Around eleven out of every 100,000 people die by suicide worldwide each year. In 2012, this translated into 804,000 fatalities.[1]

For a relatively rare event, suicide still exacts a considerable toll in absolute terms. The United Nations coordinating agency for health, the World Health Organization (WHO) recently published detailed information on suicide rates in 172 countries, some of which we have reproduced in Table 4.1. All of the rates are for 2012, although they are estimated.[2] Box 4.1 details some of the challenges associated with collecting information on this stigmatised topic.

Our table includes information from thirty of the 172 countries, which illustrates some of the main trends. There were more than 500 suicide fatalities in Ireland in 2012 and more than 43,000 in the United States. The frequency of suicide is, however, very similar in the two countries, as we can see from their suicide rates: 11.0 in Ireland and 12.1 in the United States. We use rates per 100,000 people because they allow us to accurately compare the prevalence of suicide – as well as diseases and other health conditions – between countries with different populations. Also helping us make more accurate comparisons is the fact that the rates are 'age-standardised' to account for the different age structures in different countries.

Using this measure, we find that the small South American country of Guyana can claim the unenviable status of having the world's highest suicide rate. There were 44.2 suicide deaths for every 100,000 Guyanese in 2012. Latin American and Caribbean countries typically have lower suicide rates than those in Europe, North America and Asia, so Guyana's suicide toll is an outlier among most of its neighbours. The Brazilian rate of 5.8 is much more typical of states in the region, although Guyana's neighbour, Suriname, also has a very high rate: 27.8.

In Asia, Japan, South Korea and North Korea all have elevated rates. Japan's annual number of suicide fatalities has only recently fallen below 30,000, corresponding to a rate of 18.5. Prior to this, the steady growth in its rate, from 17.6 in 1980 to 24.4 in 2009, attracted considerable attention, even in a country where suicide is sometimes seen as part of the national fabric. Such short-term changes still pale in significance, compared to what has happened in South Korea. Its rate more than quadrupled, from 6.8 in 1982 to 31.0 in 2009, before declining to 28.9 in 2012. Changing social values, economic difficulties in the late 1990s and the highly competitive nature of South Korean society are often cited as the reasons for this substantial surge in self-inflicted deaths. This competitive streak is likely to partly explain why North Korean refugees living in South Korea have a suicide rate two and a half times as large as the already colossal rate among natives of South Korea. In truth, though, the reasons for the difference are not clear. Suicides inside reclusive North Korea itself are higher than in South Korea and are only exceeded by those of Guyana.

Lithuania occupies fifth place in a league table of world suicide rates, recording a rate of 28.2, which is the highest in Europe. It is the only European country with one of the world's ten highest suicide rates, even though European countries have traditionally had higher rates than elsewhere. There is a sharp contrast between the prevalence of suicide in the north and south of the continent. Rates in Lithuania (28.2), Russia (19.5) and Finland (14.8) far exceed those of the Mediterranean states. Spain records a low rate (5.1) and the Greek rate (3.8) is Europe's second-lowest (more on this in Chapter 7). Georgia records the lowest rate (3.2) in Europe. The prevalence of suicide in Ireland (11.0) is relatively moderate, in European terms. At the same time, it is almost double that of its nearest neighbour, the United Kingdom, for reasons that are not at all clear.

In terms of absolute numbers, suicide's devastating consequences are more acutely felt in low- and middle-income countries. Between them, India and China account for roughly half of
all global suicides (47 percent). The prevalence of suicide in India
(21.1) is high by international standards, and its vast population
means that this translated into more than 258,000 suicides in
2012. China's suicide rate has declined substantially in recent
years. Between 1995 and 1999, there were an estimated 287,000
annual suicides in the country, equating to a rate of 23.2 per
100,000.[3] That China now posts a suicide rate of 'only' 7.8 per
100,000, which corresponded to a total death toll of just over
120,000 in 2012, is evidence of a dramatic change. It has been
linked to the increasing numbers of Chinese who are migrating
to cities, because suicide in China is largely a rural phenomenon.

That the suicide rate is 27.4 in Mozambique and 24.9 in
Tanzania shows that an old assumption that people kill themselves
far less frequently in Africa can be questioned. The rate in many
other African countries – such as South Africa (3.0) – is, however,
significantly lower. Almost everywhere in the Arab world, suicide
rates are spectacularly low. In 2012, only forty-three people took
their own lives in Lebanon. In the kingdom of Saudi Arabia, the
figure was ninety-eight. Both Saudi Arabia (0.4) and Lebanon (0.8)
record rates that are less than one for every 100,000 people.

Table 4.1 includes rates for 2012, but a similar table from fifty
or a hundred years ago would have shown many of these countries in similar positions. Aside from a few exceptions, national
suicide rates do not commonly show significant changes from
one year or one decade to the next. These modern patterns in
suicide rates that we describe are enduring. They show that cultural and social forces are key influences on suicide rates.

Table 4.1 | Suicide Rate and No. of Suicides, by Country (2012)

Rates are per 100,000 population, age-standardised.

Country	Rate for males and females	Rate for males	Rate for females	Number of suicides
Guyana	44.2	70.8	22.1	277
North Korea	38.5	45.4	35.1	9,790
South Korea	28.9	41.7	18.0	17,908
Sri Lanka	28.8	46.4	12.8	6,170
Lithuania	28.2	51.0	8.4	1,007
Suriname	27.8	44.5	11.9	145
Mozambique	27.4	34.2	21.1	4,360
Nepal	24.9	30.1	20.0	5,572
Tanzania	24.9	31.6	18.3	7,228
Kazakhstan	23.8	40.6	9.3	3,912
India	21.1	25.8	16.4	258,075
Russian Federation	19.5	35.1	6.2	31,997
Japan	18.5	26.9	10.1	29,442
Poland	16.6	30.5	3.8	7,848
Finland	14.8	22.2	7.5	901
El Salvador	13.6	23.5	5.7	806
USA	12.1	20.0	5.2	43,361
Thailand	11.4	19.1	4.5	8,740
Ireland	11.0	16.9	5.2	524
Argentina	10.3	17.2	4.1	4,418
China	7.8	7.1	8.7	120,730
Brazil	5.8	9.4	2.5	11,821
UK	6.2	9.8	2.6	4,360
Spain	5.1	8.2	2.2	3,296
Greece	3.8	6.3	1.3	548
South Africa	3.0	5.5	1.1	1,398
Egypt	1.7	2.4	1.2	1,264
Jamaica	1.2	1.8	0.7	33
Lebanon	0.9	1.2	0.6	43
Saudi Arabia	0.4	0.6	0.2	98

Source: Adapted from 'Preventing Suicide: A Global Imperative – Annex 1'. Geneva: WHO, 2014.

Box 4.1 | Problems with Collecting Information on Suicide

Secular authorities are no longer interested in finding out about all suicides so that they might poach the assets of those who have died. Though stigma is less prevalent now than it was in the Middle Ages, it has not disappeared. Many families still try to conceal the true cause of death, perhaps even persuading a coroner or medical examiner to record that their loved one died for some other reason. Such challenges mean that some probable suicides are concealed in official records, and that undercounting is commonplace. The Islamic view of suicide is largely condemnatory, and suicide remains criminalised in most Muslim countries. It seems plausible then that the very low rates of suicide that are reported in Arab and Muslim states are not a completely accurate reflection of how many people kill themselves.

A further difficulty is the lack of consistency regarding how suicides are recorded in different countries. In Ireland, England and Wales, coroners are responsible for reaching verdicts of suicide. Elsewhere, the opinions of the police or doctors are taken as reliable. A difficulty faced by all of these professionals is that classifying a death as suicide requires some sense of the deceased's suicidal intent. This is not an insignificant challenge and proving beyond reasonable doubt that the suicide was intentional is tougher still. One consequence of all of these hurdles is that many jurisdictions record a large number of suicides as 'of undetermined intent'. Incontrovertible proof – such as a suicide note – is left by less than half of those who end their lives. So, to require such proof before recording a death as suicide, as happens in Luxembourg, is clearly misguided.

Should we then ignore the data collected on suicide because of these reliability concerns? This would be fool-hardy, overlooking a valuable, if flawed, source of knowledge. Rather, we must recognise that undercounting occurs, factor this into all observations that rely on suicide data and constantly strive to improve accuracy – as the WHO does. The Office of National Statistics in the UK also now categorises all deaths of undetermined intent as suicides. This includes many single-vehicle road-traffic accidents, for example. Such sensible approaches should be more widely adopted.

Ireland's actual suicide death toll is likely to be higher than the roughly 500 official fatalities that are recorded in the country each year. Claims by advocates, however, that the numbers are substantially higher are likely exaggerated. They feed the myth that there is a suicide crisis in Ireland, which is not supported by the evidence. The WHO itself rates the quality of data collected in Ireland as excellent.

How? | Suicide Methods

The suicide of a British chemist attracted headlines in 2006 because he died after he drank a homemade cocktail of alcohol and chopped-up pieces of hemlock.[4] His choice of hemlock meant that he died in the same way as revered historical figures such as Socrates. Fatalities involving the poisonous plant are now extremely rare, though. Technological advancements have provided people with ways in which they can end their lives that did not exist in previous centuries: guns and pesticides, for example. Laws and regulations also influence the choices available to people who want to end it all. Were it not for liberal firearms legislation in the United States, it is unlikely that guns would be the most favoured suicide method there. Anton van Hooff's history of suicide in the ancient world highlighted how a decision to hang oneself in ancient Greece was met with disapproval.[5] He recalled how Helen of Troy once contemplated it but rejected it as not fit for a queen. Hanging was associated with the suicides of slaves and other social inferiors. Self-suffocation has, nevertheless, always been a popular suicide method.

Tables 4.2 and 4.3 show how people kill themselves in the twenty-first century in eight countries. These tables include information from multiple years, so care should be taken when interpreting the figures.

Table 4.2 | % Male Suicides, in Selected Countries, by Method

Country	Years	Other poisoning	Pesticide	Hanging	Drowning	Firearms	Falls	Other	Total Number
South Korea	1995-2004	0.4	37.5	39.2	3.2	0.4	9.5	9.8	53,449
Lithuania	1998-2004	1.1	0.4	91.7	0.3	2.7	1.3	2.4	8,778
Japan	1995-2004	1.3	2.5	68.7	2.6	0.2	8.1	16.5	199,505
USA	1999-2002	7.1	0.3	20.4	0.9	60.6	1.9	8.8	97,014
El Salvador	1997-2003	0.4	86.2	8.4	0.3	3.8	0.1	0.7	2,446
Thailand	1994-2002	6.3	16.4	51.7	0.1	6.1	0.1	19.3	27,015
Argentina	1997-2003	0.7	1.7	49.1	1.5	37.6	2.4	7.0	15,214
Great Britain	2001-2004	14.7	0.4	55.2	2.4	3.5	2.9	20.8	12,573

Source: Ajdacic-Gross, V., Weiss, M.G., Ring, M., Hepp, U., Bopp, M. and Gutzwiller, F. et al. 'Methods of Suicide: International Suicide Patterns Derived from the WHO Mortality Database. In *Bulletin of the WHO*. 2008; 86 (9): pp726-732.

Table 4.3 | % Female Suicides in Selected Countries, by Method

Country	Years	Other poisoning	Pesticides	Hanging	Drowning	Firearms	Falls	Other	Total Number
South Korea	1995-2004	0.8	42.8	26.0	3.8	0.1	18.5	8.1	23,392
Lithuania	1998-2004	6.3	1.6	83.1	2.2	0.3	4.4	2.1	1,881
Japan	1995-2004	2.9	4.3	59.9	7.8	0.0	12.5	12.7	82,646
USA	1999-2002	31.0	0.5	16.9	2.1	35.7	3.4	10.5	23,629
El Salvador	1997-2003	0.0	95.1	3.2	0.0	1.4	0.0	0.4	1,102
Thailand	1994-2002	11.3	28.3	41.8	0.1	1.9	0.2	16.4	8,669
Argentina	1997-2003	3.4	4.1	38.0	4.2	25.9	10.3	14.1	4,188
Great Britain	2001-2004	41.1	0.3	35.9	4.7	0.6	3.7	13.9	3,832

Source: Ajdacic-Gross, V., Weiss, M.G., Ring, M., Hepp, U., Bopp, M., Gutzwiller, F. et al. 2008.

Hanging was the most common way people ended their lives in the countries included in tables 4.2 and 4.3, although its popularity differed from one country to the next. More than nine out of ten men and eight out of ten women from Lithuania who killed themselves chose hanging. In contrast, fewer than one in ten men and one in thirty women from El Salvador used this method. Around half of male suicide deaths in Argentina, Great Britain and Thailand were as a result of hanging.

Death by hanging was so low in El Salvador because of the enormous contribution to suicide mortality made by the world's most common suicide method: pesticide self-poisoning. Death from pesticide poisoning is especially agonising, and people commonly die days after the initial suicidal act. Nevertheless, it was the method chosen by 86.2 percent of Salvadoran men who committed suicide and a startling 95.1 percent of Salvadoran women. Pesticides make a notable but much smaller contribution in South Korea and, to a lesser extent, in Thailand. In the other five developed countries, the impact of pesticides was pretty insignificant. The third column of both tables shows the category 'Other poisoning', which includes easily available medications such as paracetamol, as well as illicit drugs. This category makes a larger contribution to suicide mortality in developed countries, especially for women. Four in every ten British women who died by suicide did so using such drugs.

The United States contrasts starkly with the other selected countries because of the substantial proportion of suicides that involve firearms. More than three out of every five American men who took their own lives used guns, as did around a third of American female suicide victims. Of the other selected countries, only in Argentina were firearms commonly used by people to take their own lives. The sheer scale of suicide involving guns in the United States and pesticides in El Salvador shows how easy access to a lethal means of suicide can have a profound influence on the way in which people kill themselves.

Who? Age and Gender

Fortunately, young children rarely take their own lives. It is only during adolescence that we see young people begin to kill themselves. Distressing as this is, and in spite of media interest in adolescent suicides, especially after a cluster of suicide deaths, the prevalence of teenage suicide is not especially high worldwide. Usually, the older we get, the more likely we become to kill ourselves. This is especially true in Asian countries. South Koreans over the age of sixty-five are more than four times as likely to end their lives as those younger than thirty-five.

This global picture of the relationship between age and suicide does not hold true for all countries. Ireland is different from many other countries because of the high incidence of suicide among young males. Whereas male rates worldwide usually peak in the oldest age groups, they are high among Irish men between the ages of fifteen and twenty-nine. Slightly higher rates are found among those between the ages of thirty and forty-nine. In sharp contrast to the situation in South Korea, Irish men aged fifteen to forty-nine are more than twice as likely as those over the age of seventy to end their own lives. As younger men do not typically die from the cancers and heart diseases that claim the lives of many older people, suicide is the leading killer of younger men in Ireland.

Figure 4.1 | Worldwide Suicide Rates, 2008 Estimates

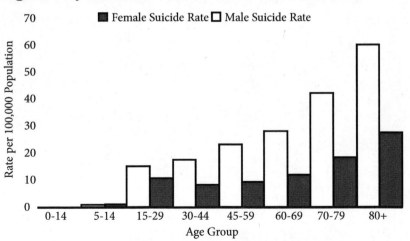

Source: Varnik, P. 'Suicide in the World'. In *International Journal of Environmental Research and Public Health.* 2012; 9: pp760-771.

It is unsurprising, then, that much of the Irish media demonstrates a sustained interest in these deaths. The problem with this obsession, however, is that such reporting frequently conveys the impression that there is a suicide crisis in Ireland. That young men are dying in such circumstances is tragic, of course, but we must convey an accurate picture of suicide in the country as a whole. The data unequivocally shows that, by international standards, the overall rate of suicide in Ireland is not especially high.

What we also see in this graph is the well-established pattern of more men killing themselves than women. China is one of the few countries in the world where women kill themselves at a greater rate than men (see Box 4.2). In most European and American countries, men are between two and four times more likely than women to kill themselves. Men are also much more likely to take their own lives in most of Asia, although the gap is not as large as elsewhere.

So what is going on with men? Firstly, we know that a higher proportion of men kill themselves than women, but that women account for more suicide *attempts*. One reason men are more 'successful' when they try to kill themselves is because of their preference for more violent and lethal methods, such as hanging and guns. Women prefer drugs or poisons, and these just do not kill as often or as fast. The baseline tendency of men to suicidality also tends to be higher, because socialisation leaves them more exposed and habituated to all types of violence than women.

Romantic relationships – and marriage, in particular – also provide men with a protective blanket against suicide, and when these are absent or end abruptly, men can be especially vulnerable. Joan Freeman, the chief executive of Pieta House, a suicide-prevention agency that operates all over Ireland, emphasises how

difficult men find it to cope with the loss of a significant relationship. When relationships end, social isolation often results,
which can be experienced as deeply traumatic. Women will usually have wider social networks and more close friends. Freeman
expands on the situation that confronts a lot of Irish men:

> Well, the chances are, he's got to be the one who's to leave the
> family home. So, he's lost his home, he's lost the woman that he
> loves. More than likely, they shared a circle of friends, you know
> – enforced isolation. He's probably living in a little flat some-
> where, you know, but the worst part of all is losing that sponta-
> neous access to his children. He is punished from the moment
> the relationship is over until the end.[6]

When men find themselves in such a predicament, they are also
far less likely to seek help. Freeman was pleasantly surprised
when, shortly after the opening of Pieta House, she realised that
almost half of the people availing of the service were men. She
later discovered that it was almost always women who made the
appointments for them. Many men prefer to tough it out when
facing a problem and regard reaching out for help as an act of
cowardice, which is alien to their concept of masculinity. This
means they feel the stress of challenging life events more acutely,
which contributes to an escalation of suicide risk. Professor Ella
Arensman believes that, even when they are very depressed or
coping with other issues, women are more likely to pick up the
phone and keep trying for a solution.[7]

Men's greater tendency to impulsivity and aggressiveness,
often under the influence of alcohol, is also relevant. It means
some men are less capable of resolving predicaments in a non-
impulsive, non-aggressive way. This is linked to their preference
for more-lethal suicide methods. Women are likely to be more

ambiguous about dying. If you swallow a lot of pills, you will not die immediately. There is a decent chance you will be discovered by someone before it is too late. Change your mind after ingesting the drugs and you may still have time to get to a hospital. Not so for a man who has shot himself.

In spite of the greater prevalence of suicide amongst men, we must not forget that women can and do kill themselves. The highest rates among females in Ireland are found amongst middle-aged women. Freeman links this to the losses that many women of this age experience. Their children have likely grown up and moved on. Their confidence may have been dented by the ending of a relationship or a loss of youthfulness.[8] Still, suicide rates among middle-aged women in Ireland remain lower than for men of any age group. As we mentioned earlier, one of the few countries in the world where the suicide rate for women exceeds that for men is China.

Box 4.2 | Female Suicide in China

Why do more Chinese women kill themselves than men? The Chinese ethical system of Confucianism is often blamed. Chinese women are constantly reminded of their inferior position in society, through the universal preference for male children, for example. Such norms may contribute to women perceiving themselves as burdens. The state's one-child policy may also play a role.

What is clear is that social factors are more relevant in suicide fatalities in China than in the West; only around half of Chinese suicides are associated with mental illness. Marriage does not protect Chinese women against fatal self-injury, as it does elsewhere. China remains a deeply conservative society

---

and the experience of marital problems against this backdrop may explain why some women seek escape through suicide. China is also thought to have high levels of domestic violence.

Suicide in China is primarily a rural problem, with rates in rural areas between two and five times as high as in cities. And it is in rural areas that highly lethal agricultural chemicals are available to the large numbers of women who work in agriculture. Most rural Chinese households store these chemicals. Drugs such as paracetamol, which are used in suicide attempts in the West, can kill, but far less frequently. Overdoses of paracetamol result in death less than 1 percent of the time; if ingested, the herbicide paraquat kills 60 percent of the time. Access to the emergency medical care that is so vital after an episode of self-poisoning is unavailable outside of China's urban areas.

Pesticides were used in some 62 percent of suicides in China between 1996 and 2002.[9] When a distressed Chinese woman reaches for a pesticide to swallow, her suicidal intent is likely not very different from the Western woman who reaches for paracetamol. Access to a highly lethal means of suicide is a crucial factor, then, which contributes to the large numbers of Chinese women who kill themselves.

Sub-national Suicide Trends

A broad survey of national and international suicide trends inevitably obscures distinctive local patterns and variations among groups within countries. Ethnicity is important. In the United States, white people kill themselves more often than

Hispanic Americans and black Americans. In New Zealand and Australia, the Maori and Aboriginal populations have higher suicide rates than those of European descent. China and India both have higher rates in rural areas than in towns and cities.

Dr John Connolly, who co-founded the Irish Association of Suicidology in 1996, worked with four colleagues to explore suicide trends in two Irish counties, Kildare and Mayo, between 1988 and 1994.[10] They found that the ways that people end their lives are influenced by local factors. For example, around half of men (46 percent) and women (52 percent) in Mayo who killed themselves died by drowning, which is a relatively uncommon suicide method in Ireland. In Kildare, 23 percent of men who took their own lives in Kildare used guns, also an atypical method in the country as a whole. Mayo is a coastal county with a large number of rivers and lakes and Kildare has a large military facility. Further analysis of information collected in Kildare showed that more than 60 percent of the men who killed themselves with a firearm there were employed by the army.

If we are to understand more about suicide where we live and in the groups we belong to, we cannot just rely on national trends. But we must be wary of misunderstanding natural variance in the incidence of suicide among small populations, in towns or counties or among patients of a particular mental-health service. Because the base rate of suicide is so low, the expectation, from a statistical perspective, is that there will be wide variations in the prevalence of suicide in a small population in any given period. The vast majority of the time, this should not be a cause of panic or obsession, necessitating investigation and the assignment of blame. Rather, it should be recognised for what it is: a temporary, random rate increase.

*

By poring over the available data on any phenomenon, we come to understand more about it. Suicide is no exception. Myths that are associated with voluntary death can be corrected. In Ireland, the obsession with the supposedly large numbers of people dying by suicide would lead you to believe that, compared to suicide rates in other countries, Irish suicide rates are extraordinary. They are, in fact, relatively moderate. Every country is likely to have a high incidence amongst some particular group. This is true of older white men in the United States, indigenous groups in many countries and young men in Ireland. We do not mean to diminish the distressing impact that suicide has on the bereaved. A rational analysis must prevail, however.

Ultimately, the hope is that by understanding more about suicide, we can prevent more suicides. Our earlier finding that easy access to lethal methods of suicide influences how people kill themselves indicates opportunities to prevent some deaths by restricting access to such methods. We will explore this in more detail and take an in-depth look at suicide-prevention later. Yet, as we have seen, powerful social and cultural forces shape a country's suicide rates. Such forces are resistant to change, which means that preventing suicides will never be easy.

5.
Misunderstanding Suicide, a Case Study: Ireland's Abortion Legislation

In 2013, Ireland's parliament, the Oireachtas, passed the Protection of Life During Pregnancy Act. The law provides for an unusual connection between two issues that span ethics and public policy: abortion and suicide. In a country that has some of the strictest abortion laws in the world, one of the limited circumstances in which a woman can now access an abortion is when doctors conclude that there is a substantial risk that she will kill herself. Prior to the passage of the legislation, it was difficult to escape debates between those in favour of it and those opposed to it. Television, radio, newspapers and posters across the country also provided analysis of the connections between suicide and abortion.

An average citizen who, in spite of all this, failed to grasp some of the critical facts about such complex issues can be forgiven. However, we are entitled to expect our politicians to fare a little better. Pro-life and pro-choice stances on abortion, as well as the nature of politics, clearly complicate this issue. But we contend that the law's provisions concerning the connections between suicide and abortion should have largely reflected current evidence.

Irish politicians cannot claim that they were not well-informed on all of the issues. In addition to the easily available public information, parliamentary committees heard evidence and received submissions from a wide range of experts and advocacy groups. The resultant law rests, however, on a number of shaky assumptions that relate to suicide.

★

Abortion has been a minefield for Ireland's politicians for decades. Though outlawed since the nineteenth century, the worst fear of pro-life groups in the early 1980s was that a liberal interpretation of Ireland's Constitution might allow abortion to be legalised through the back door. A campaign to introduce a constitutional prohibition on abortion culminated in a 'pro-life amendment' being introduced to the Constitution in 1983, after it was approved by the Irish people in a referendum.

Judicial interpretation of this article took centre stage in 1992, when the legal adviser to the Irish government, the attorney general, sought a High Court injunction to prevent 'Miss X', a fourteen-year-old girl, from travelling to Britain for an abortion. That the teenage girl had become pregnant as a result of rape ensured that Ireland's restrictive abortion laws attracted global attention, especially when the High Court granted an interim injunction.

This decision was immediately appealed to Ireland's Supreme Court. Of central importance to the Supreme Court's consideration was evidence of the girl's stated intention to kill herself if she were forced to continue with the pregnancy. The controversial majority decision of the court was that the 'pro-life amendment' to the Constitution actually provides for a right to abortion where, as a matter of probability, there is a real and substantial risk to the life of the mother and the only means of removing that risk is termination of the pregnancy. Miss X was subsequently allowed to travel to Britain with her parents for a termination.

Reasoned constitutional arguments were put forward by the Supreme Court judges for their decision, but the fact that they never heard any medical evidence as to the risk of the girl killing herself or the nature of abortion as a treatment for suicidality means that the decision has always been discredited among Ireland's vocal pro-life movement.

Though the Supreme Court decision established that abortion is legal in Ireland, albeit in very limited circumstances, Human Rights Watch reported in 2010 that it had not been able to document a single case of a legal termination of a pregnancy as provided for by the X-case judgment.[1] This does not mean, though, that abortion is unfamiliar to Irish women. Between 1980 and 2012, more than 156,000 Irish women accessed abortion services abroad, mainly in the UK.[2] Ireland has effectively exported its unwanted pregnancy problem, and successive Irish governments have been, until recently, content to avoid introducing legislation on the issue.

A ruling from the European Court of Human Rights in 2009 finally forced an Irish government to take action. The court found that Ireland had breached human rights norms by not establishing accessible and effective procedures for pregnant women to access abortion services in line with the law, i.e. where there is a real and substantial risk to their lives. The Irish government established an expert group in 2012 to examine options for implementing the court's findings. After considering the expert group's findings, the government decided to introduce legislation to clarify the circumstances in which abortion could be provided.

The result, the Protection of Life During Pregnancy Act 2013, took effect in January 2014. Abortion remains illegal in Ireland in most circumstances but, in line with the 1992 Supreme Court judgement, the law clarifies that abortion is now permitted where there is a risk to the life of the mother. Three doctors – an obstetrician and two psychiatrists – must concur that there is a real and substantial risk to the woman's life.

Four questionable assumptions underpin this legislation. It assumes that:

1. A not-insignificant number of suicidal pregnant women will go on to kill themselves unless they are granted abortions;

2. Doctors can identify those pregnant women who are at risk of killing themselves unless provided with access to a termination;

3. Abortion can be an effective intervention for someone who is suicidal; and

4. It is very unlikely that large numbers of pregnant women will feign suicidal ideation and mislead psychiatrists so that they might be granted access to abortions.

We will examine each of these assumptions in turn.

Suicide Risk Among Pregnant Women

We have already shown that there is very little chance of a person with suicidal ideas going on to kill themself. Might it be different for a woman with an unplanned pregnancy who presents to a doctor with suicidal ideation? Approximately a hundred women kill themselves in Ireland each year. Reliable information that is collected on suicides amongst pregnant women comes from the UK. It shows that pregnancy has a profound protective effect against suicide. Only around one in every 500,000 British women who were pregnant between 2006 and 2008 ended their lives, which corresponds to a suicide rate twenty times lower than that found among other women.[3] The majority of suicides associated with pregnancy actually happen after a woman has given birth.

Unlike the situation in Ireland, access to abortion services for British women is relatively straightforward. Restrictive abortion laws at home and the resulting difficulties associated with seeking a termination abroad may, of course, lead to more distress among Irish women who have to deal with unwanted pregnancies. Costs and travel restrictions also create real barriers for certain groups of women living in Ireland, such as low-income groups and asylum seekers. Still, as thousands of Irish women have managed to access abortion services abroad for decades, we suggest that the number of women unable to access a termination abroad is negligible.

Irish women are twice as likely as British women to end their lives. This is not, however, sufficient reason for us to suppose that suicide rates among pregnant Irish women follow a substantially different pattern to suicide rates among pregnant British women. It is safe to assume that suicide among pregnant Irish women is less common than among non-pregnant Irish women, as is the case in Britain. And so the likelihood of a pregnant woman, Irish or otherwise, with a planned or unplanned pregnancy killing herself is pretty remote.

Predicting Suicide Among Pregnant Women

Doctors are also unable to adequately assess for suicide risk or predict suicide among psychiatric patients. There is no reason why this should be any different for pregnant women who present with suicidal ideation. The law's assumption that two psychiatrists and an obstetrician will be able to identify which pregnant women are at real risk of ending their lives is unsound. In an effort to assist health professionals in dealing with the new law, Ireland's Department of Health produced guidelines. Amnesty Ireland, however, insisted that the guidelines 'fail miserably to address the most pressing issue of the Act – how exactly medical professionals are to assess when a pregnancy poses a "real and substantial" risk to the life of a woman or girl'.[4]

Abortion as an Effective Intervention for Suicidal Women

It is possible that granting a suicidal pregnant woman access to an abortion might make her less likely to kill herself. Among professionals who appeared before the Oireachtas committee, there were clear differences of opinion. Professor Patricia Casey, a consultant psychiatrist, claimed that abortion is not a cure for suicidal risk, and that to allow abortion in such circumstances would open the floodgates and lead to a liberal abortion regime in Ireland. Professor Veronica O'Keane, also a consultant psychiatrist, suggested that there will be women who are actively suicidal on the basis of their pregnancy alone and that an abortion will render them safe.

There is no reliable information on the impact of abortion on suicide risk. What is available, though, is an imperfect proxy measure that has assessed the impact of abortion on women's mental health.[5] A detailed review published by the Academy of Royal Medical Colleges in the UK in 2011 found that an unwanted pregnancy was associated with an increased risk of mental-health problems. Rates of mental-health problems for women in such a situation are largely similar, though, whether they have an abortion or give birth. There is no evidence, then, to support a claim that abortion has a negative impact on a woman's mental health.

As the outcomes, in terms of mental health, for women with unwanted pregnancies who gave birth and had terminations were the same, equally it cannot be concluded that abortion is an effective treatment for women with mental-health problems. It would be preferable if information were available on the impact of abortion on suicidal ideation and suicidal behaviour as distinct from mental illness. This finding, at the very least, calls into question the theory that abortion will cure women of being suicidal.

Malingering

A further controversial aspect of Ireland's abortion law is the suggestion that pregnant women might pretend to be suicidal so that they might be granted an abortion. The idea so troubled the pro-choice Irish Family Planning Association that it branded such claims 'profoundly disrespectful'.[6] Dr Rhona O'Mahony, a consultant obstetrician and master of Ireland's National Maternity Hospital, was personally offended by 'pejorative and judgemental views that women will manipulate doctors in order to obtain terminations of pregnancies on the basis of fabricated ideas of suicidal ideation or intent'.[7] In contrast, the College of Psychiatrists of Ireland recognised the reality of illness deception and acknowledged that a small number of people will manipulate doctors. Much faith is placed in the sincerity of Irish women faced with crisis pregnancies.

How likely is it that a woman might manipulate doctors in such a situation? Historical examples of people feigning illness to achieve their goals abound. In particular, generations of men eager to shirk the dangers of military duty have shown themselves capable of deploying all manner of illness-related avoidance tactics. During the First World War, some soldiers deliberately stuck arms and legs over trenches so that they might be shot by enemy troops, and military men with genuine illnesses were able to sell specimens of their afflictions to otherwise healthy colleagues.[8]

The work of sociologist Walter Sulzbach shows that following the introduction of social insurance in Germany in the nineteenth century, sick leave soared. In 1885, the year of its introduction, the average number of sick days taken by a German worker was 14.1. At the turn of the twentieth century, it was 17.6. By 1940, it was 30.0.[9] All of this happened during a fifty-year period in which public health was rapidly improving because of greater access to health services and advances in medicine. Of course, many Germans were simply taking advantage of a system that had not previously existed. So it is clear that people will lie about medical conditions in order to achieve their goals.

Even if a doctor identifies or suspects that a woman is feigning an illness or condition – suicidal ideation, for example – that doctor may not necessarily try to prevent her from accessing 'appropriate' treatment, such as an abortion. The data available on the reasons for abortions obtained by Irish women in Britain suggests that pregnant Irish women, in collusion with British doctors, are involved in deception. Ninety-five percent of British abortions involving Irish women were granted on the basis that 'the continuation of the pregnancy would involve risk, greater than if the pregnancy were terminated, of injury to the physical or mental health of the pregnant woman'.[10] This remarkably high figure led the largest provider of abortions in Britain, the British Pregnancy Advisory Service, to conclude that in most cases in which women cite a risk to their mental health as the grounds for the abortion, this is not necessarily true. Rather, women and doctors are compelled to indicate that it is, because of the nature of the abortion laws in Britain.[11]

Of course, some Irish women will present with genuine suicidal ideation if they see abortion as the only solution to their predicament, and we know that an unwanted pregnancy in itself does negatively affect the mental health of many women. Still, given the many historical and contemporary examples of illness deception, the possibility that doctors may collude in granting abortions, and the clear opportunity for primary gain in the form of access to abortion as a solution to a crisis pregnancy, we respectfully suggest that any notion that some Irish women will not feign suicidal ideation to access abortion is far-fetched. The temptation is there for a woman with a crisis pregnancy to exaggerate the suicidal aspect. This is human nature, it is universal and not everybody will resist.

★

Four shaky assumptions, then, underpin Ireland's recent abortion law. If the Protection of Life During Pregnancy Act results in anything more than a very small number (in the single digits) of Irish women being granted terminations in any year, it will be because of inaccurate assessments of suicide risk. These are common. In clinical practice, the threshold for belief that a patient may pose a genuine risk of suicide is usually quite low, resulting in a sizeable proportion of admissions to psychiatric hospitals. Many psychiatrists inappropriately hospitalise patients who present with suicidal ideation, and we can expect doctors to play it safe when implementing this legislation by concurring that there is a genuine risk of suicide, even though this cannot be accurately deduced.

There are consequences, however, to the state sanctioning an inaccurate understanding of suicide, which should concern all of us. Can we reasonably expect the state to introduce other evidence-based policies that relate to suicide when, on this occasion, evidence was at best not taken sufficiently into account and, at worst, blatantly ignored? And what of the risks associated with conveying inaccurate messages about suicide to the general public? In an ideal world, suicidal threat would not be grounds for termination of a pregnancy, but, in our imperfect situation, we need to guard against suicide risk becoming an acceptable reason for obtaining a range of benefits. Furthermore, popularising the language of suicide can lead to more suicides, an issue we will examine in more detail in Chapter 8.

6.
Suicide Stories

Behind the facts and figures of suicide are real people – fathers, mothers, sons, daughters and friends – who have taken their own lives. Countless more are left behind to grieve. By exploring the stories of suicide victims, we can put faces to some of the people captured in the statistics. We can also gain some small insight into the fear and anxiety that confronts a person before they decide to carry out the ultimate act of self-destruction.

A different type of anxiety is likely to have entered the lives of those close to them before such a death. Suicides are frequently preceded by one or more suicide attempts, which leave friends and families wondering if there will be another – and whether it will be successful. Tragically, it sometimes is, and loved ones then have to bear the distinctive pain associated with self-inflicted death.

Here we will examine five accounts of people who took their own lives. The suicides of modern celebrities are like those of ancient Greek and Roman aristocrats. Their celebrity status attracts considerable attention, and such deaths are examined in more detail than the suicides of people who are less well-known. Robert Enke and Ernest Hemingway are two such celebrity suicides.

Enke was a successful professional footballer whose November 2009 death sent shockwaves through Germany and beyond. He believed his status meant that he could only reveal his depression to his family, close friends and some clinicians. Since his death, his wife Teresa has talked openly about his struggles and cooperated with Ronald Reng, who has written a moving account of the goalkeeper's ups and downs on and off the football pitch.[1]

Hemingway, the celebrated writer, was also reluctant to reveal his mental-health difficulties – and even more unwilling than Enke to seek treatment. What set Hemingway apart from Enke and many other people who take their own lives was the presence of so many of the known risk factors for suicide. He had a life-long history of mental-health problems, came from a family with a history of suicide, experienced an unhappy childhood, was dependent on alcohol, had various physical ailments, had relationship problems and had made three prior suicide attempts.

Aside from the stories of Enke and Hemingway, we will also examine the stories of Sean Quinn, Shane D'Alton and Michael McNamara, three less well-known Dubliners. John Quinn and Eddie Dalton, the fathers of Sean and Shane, and Phyllis McNamara, Michael's wife, told their moving stories to Carl O'Brien of the *Irish Times* as part of that paper's Stories of Suicide series of November 2010.[2] All three have since dedicated much of their time to preventing others from taking their own lives.

Robert Enke

More than 45,000 people attended the funeral of professional footballer Robert Enke, following his 10 November 2009 suicide. Many of them would have expected him to be Germany's number-one goalkeeper at the 2010 World Cup. What football fans and Enke's coaches and teammates did not know was that he had periodically struggled with depression and anxiety for much of his professional career.

After leaving Germany to join Benfica of Portugal in 1999, he suffered a panic attack on the day he signed his contract; as a result, his official unveiling as a player was cancelled. During his time with Barcelona, in 2002 and 2003, he only started three games. Following a poor performance in a cup defeat against a team from the third-tier of Spanish football, Enke's self-doubt tormented him. His first definite period of clinical depression began – and he began seeing a psychologist.

Enke's next season started with a loan move to the Turkish team Fenerbahçe, but disaster struck in his first game. He made a number of errors and Fenerbahçe's unforgiving fans blamed him for the 3-0 defeat. Coins, lighters and bottles rained down on him, and he was despondent after the game. Two months after breaking his contract and leaving Istanbul, he wrote an entry in his diary which began with the words, 'About to go mad', and ended with 'Often think about . . .'[3] No suicidal acts accompanied Enke's suicidal thoughts this time, but his deep depression remained for a further three months.

Enke's mood lifted following some recuperation, and a return to his native Germany with Hannover 96 saw him recapture some of his best form. To those who knew him well, he seemed to cope extraordinarily well following the tragic death in 2006 of his two-year-old daughter Lara, who had been born with a rare heart defect. Success on the field continued, and his teammates elected him captain of Hannover prior to the start of the 2007-2008 season. His football redemption appeared complete shortly afterwards, when he established himself as the national team's first-choice keeper.

The depression that he had shaken off more than four years earlier returned, however. Enke struggled to understand why, when he was enjoying so much success on the field, depression would take hold of him again. Its emergence during a difficult period with Barcelona had at least made some sense.

At the start of the 2009-2010 season, one of Enke's teammates noticed that his captain withdrew to his room after training. He also preferred to practice alone, with Hannover's goalkeeping coach. He complained that he constantly felt tired. At a training camp for the national team in Cologne in September 2009, Enke's anxiety was acute. He could not sleep and struggled just to talk to the other players. He continued to speak to his psychologist, but noted in his diary that he was not honest with him.

On 6 September 2009, Enke admitted to his wife that he had driven all through Cologne, looking for a spot where he could kill himself. He pulled out of the national squad the next morning. The media were told that he had a mysterious infection. At this point, he pondered whether he should make his depression public or seek treatment in a clinic. His wife subsequently confirmed that he feared that if people found out, his career would be at an end. He also fretted that social services would take the couple's adopted daughter away.

Somehow, in the midst of all this, Enke returned to playing for his club. He continued to receive treatment in his final days, but refused to be admitted to a private psychiatric clinic, saying 'I'm an international goalkeeper. I can't go to a clinic.'[4]

In Enke's last days, his wife, Teresa, thought he was in a better mood. They went to their favourite spot in Hannover, a café, on the day before his death. Enke's suicide note sought forgiveness for disguising his true mood in these final days. Not every suicidal decision is impulsive, and his disguised mood may have indicated an inner relief at having finally made the decision to kill himself. This is a phenomenon that has been reported by other relatives of suicides.

The next day, Enke pretended that he had arranged an extra training session. After driving around for eight hours, he stepped in front of an express train at 6.15 PM.

Ernest Hemingway

Ernest Hemingway died after he shot himself on 2 July 1961. Nobel and Pulitzer prizes testified to his brilliance as an author. Other interests included a passion for bullfighting, which radiates through his novel, *The Sun Also Rises*, which famously depicts the San Fermín bull-running festival. There is a monument to Hemingway in Pamplona, recognising his love of the pursuit. Deep-sea fishing and safari hunting were other less-than-mundane interests that allowed Hemingway to present a macho image to the world. Hemingway, however, had multiple vulnerabilities, which allow us to see his life in a very different way from the face that he presented to the world.

Hemingway's childhood contained many painful memories. His father, Clarence, enforced strict discipline at home and regularly beat the young Ernest, sometimes with a razor strap. Ernest was filled with rage and imagined himself shooting dead his father in revenge. Christopher Martin has sketched a psychological portrait of Hemingway, using information from his letters and the multiple biographies that have been written about him.[5] He speculates that Hemingway's father's eventual suicide may have left Ernest full of guilt, because he had imagined killing him. Whatever Hemingway's feelings for his father were, though, he saved his most severe criticism for his mother. We know that he resented her fondness for dressing him as a girl when he was a child. His loathing for her persisted throughout his life.

Lest Ernest forget how his father had died, some years later, his mother sent him the gun that his father had used to kill himself. This may have served as a reminder that, in the Hemingway family, suicide was an acceptable solution to problems. The means by which Ernest too could kill himself was also easily available. The frequency of suicide in the Hemingway family, though, suggests that the Hemingway genes may contain a strong biological predisposition to suicide. Ernest's sister, Ursula, and brother, Leicester, also took their own lives, and suicide was the suspected cause of death for another sister, Marcelline, although her death was officially regarded as having been due to natural causes. Skip forward a couple of generations and Ernest's granddaughter, Margaux, also killed herself.

Hemingway wrote to his mother-in-law in 1936 that his own experience of what he called 'melancholia' made him more tolerant of what had happened to his father. Martin concludes that while Hemingway was admitting a depressive episode, the evidence of other periods in his life during which an elevated mood was reported suggests that his illness was more likely a bipolar disorder. Hemingway's biographies are full of examples in which he is full of energy, which made his company difficult to tolerate. During these periods, his writing output was ferocious. He quickly put together seven short stories during such an episode in 1924. Paranoid delusions followed in later life, and he convinced himself that the FBI was monitoring him. During a stay in a psychiatric hospital in 1960, he underwent a course of electroconvulsive therapy.

Added to Hemingway's mental illness was an array of physical health problems. He was overweight, and had a high cholesterol level and a chronic bad back. He was also incredibly accident prone. In the space of two months in 1954, he suffered a string of serious injuries. He sustained a sprained shoulder in a plane crash. He received multiple injuries, including a fractured skull, a crushed vertebra and a ruptured liver, spleen and kidney when he was involved in an emergency evacuation from the replacement aircraft, using his head as a battering ram. The following month, he added second-degree burns to his legs, chest, lips, left hand and forearm to his battle scars, when he fell while helping to extinguish a fire.

Hemingway abused alcohol for most of his adult life, and his drinking exploits were legendary. When he was a teenager recovering from an injury received during the First World War, hospital staff found cognac bottles in his hospital room. His fondness for drinking in hospitals had not disappeared some twenty-seven years later when his then wife, Martha Gellhorn, found empty alcohol bottles under his bed while he was recovering from a car accident. Doctors pleaded with Hemingway to stop drinking and, despite recognising that he should limit his intake, he was never able to stay sober for any extended period of time.

In 1961, the year of his death, Hemingway made three suicide attempts in the space of four days. He was initially interrupted by his wife as he was loading a gun and was immediately admitted to the local psychiatric hospital in Ketchum, Idaho. He persuaded the hospital staff to allow him to go home to pick up some personal belongings, only to escape from their clutches. He managed to grab a shotgun, which he pointed at himself and was only just prevented by the staff from using. En route to the Mayo

Clinic for further psychiatric treatment a few days later, he made for the aircraft's propeller. Some quick thinking by the pilot, who cut the engine, thwarted this effort.[6]

Added to Hemingway's difficult childhood, the family history of mental and physical illness and previous suicide attempts were serious relationship problems. These were certainly not confined to difficulties getting on with his parents. He was married four times and his disagreeable personality meant that he quarrelled regularly with friends. Work difficulties are also associated with many suicides and, in spite of his status as a world-renowned writer, Ernest was unhappy with the quality of his writing output in later years.

Ernest's granddaughter Mariel was born in 1961, a few months after Ernest killed himself. A talented actress, she was nominated for a Global Globe for her performance in the Woody Allen movie, *Manhattan*. She has described her own experiences of depression and suicidal ideation as *Running from Crazy*, the title of the 2013 documentary in which she chronicles the legacy of mental illness within the family. She is now a powerful advocate for suicide prevention.

John Quinn

John Quinn is a taxi driver from the working-class community of Clondalkin, in West Dublin. His seventeen-year-old son Sean took his own life in 2005. John recalled to Carl O'Brien how he had noticed that Sean had not quite been himself for months before the first confirmation that something serious was wrong. One evening, an emotional Sean admitted to having tried to kill himself by taking an overdose. John assured his son that they would solve the problem together.

Thus began the Quinns' frustrating interaction with the Irish health system. They had to wait seven weeks to access a counselling service for teenagers, but Sean's suicidal feelings continued. This prompted John to bring him to the local accident-and-emergency service, which led to a referral to an addiction service. This was not what Sean needed. Complaints to a consultant psychiatrist led to an undertaking that Sean's GP would be advised to release him into the consultant's care. The letter never arrived, though, only convincing John even further that the system was letting them down.

What also unnerved John was that Sean was never quite able to explain why he was feeling the way he was. He did not exhibit the typical symptoms of depression, as he stayed in contact with his friends, who thought he was the same as ever. His suicide attempt and recurring suicidal feelings, nevertheless, meant that John kept a close eye on Sean. Father and son also came to an agreement. Sean promised his father that he would call him if he ever felt like taking his life again. He had seen a counsellor a few times, and John even allowed himself to think that the worse phase of the crisis might be over.

Returning from the pub one evening with his wife, John found Sean hanging. He recounts the aftermath:

> The ambulance came and they took him away on his own. That's when reality hit. I knew he was dead. I just screamed. My son had to slap me in the face to get me to my senses. I fell on the ground and just kept screaming.[7]

Anger, guilt and sadness consumed John in the immediate aftermath of Sean's death. The trauma of Sean's suicide left its mark on the Quinn family in different ways. One of John's sons could only sleep for a couple of hours a night. His other son, who played football semi-professionally, quit the game. John's wife cried day after day. John had to stop driving his taxi for a few months. Sean's suicide also deeply affected his friends.

John reckons that he attended thirteen funerals of people who took their own lives in 2005. The devastation caused by all of these deaths created a burning desire within him to prevent others from dying by suicide. His quest began on the day of Sean's funeral, as he addressed the church congregation and pleaded with other young people in the area. 'There's no need to do this – suicide is not an answer to your problems. If you feel you've no one to talk to, come to me.'[8] Many young people heeded John's call. He told O'Brien that young men in crisis picked up the phone to talk to him or arrived at his house unexpectedly most weeks.

One such young man was Damian Martin, who tried to kill himself by driving through Dublin city centre at high speed in 2008. Alerted to John's availability by his parents, Damian credited John with convincing him to view his problems differently, and helping him to understand that suicide is a permanent solution to a temporary problem. He sought help at Pieta House, a nationwide service offering treatment to suicidal persons (see Box 6.1 below). Damian has since been leading a normal life.

John attributes the decrease in the number of deaths due to suicide in the Clondalkin area in recent years to the fact that many people in crisis are now attending Pieta House. Yet the setting up of centres like Pieta House will not in itself tackle the problem of suicide, according to John. He believes that there is a role for everyone – that we all need to be aware of suicide, its risk factors and the variety of sources of help.

Shane D'Alton

Like many Irish people in their twenties before him, Eddie D'Alton's son, Shane, decided to travel to Australia in 2008. As a qualified electrician, he could have expected to find work easily. He was blessed with an outgoing personality and his girlfriend was based in Australia, so his family had no reason to worry as he set off.

Shane mainly spent his first few weeks partying. Then, all of a sudden, an upset Shane rang home and said he wanted to come home. Eddie met Shane at the airport, where he found his son crying and almost unrecognisable. When Shane was diagnosed with depression and prescribed medication by his GP, Eddie was surprised. He guessed that Shane was just feeling sorry for himself because he had had to leave Australia early, or that maybe he had just been homesick.

Shane returned to Australia after securing a job, but only a week after his return, another phone call from Australia revealed that all was still not well. After spending a night drinking, he had been mugged, injured and brought to hospital, where the main medical concern was his depression. Eddie immediately set off for Australia.

> I remember the doctor saying: "We take depression very seriously in this country – in six weeks, we can sort it out if you leave him here with us." I thought about it, but it was close to Christmas. I figured he'd be better off at home, surrounded by family and friends. He had medical insurance, so he'd be bound to get decent treatment. Looking back, that was a big mistake.[9]

After Sean returned home again, he revealed a previous suicide attempt, in which he had cut himself. He promised his father he would not to do it again. He was admitted to an inpatient mental-health facility in Dublin, but his whole experience there shocked his father. Eddie just could not see how spending time in the midst of so many other visibly unwell people could help Sean to get better.

The speed at which treatment was forthcoming was a major source of frustration for the D'Altons, just as it had been for John Quinn. A number of days after being promised that a psychologist would review Shane's case, it still had not happened. After a week, he still had not even been seen by a psychiatrist. Shane's condition seemed to be getting worse, but a decision was still taken to discharge him over a weekend.

Shane's parents went out for dinner that Saturday night and, when they returned, a comment from family members that Shane had been snoring loudly set off alarm bells – Shane did not normally snore. It turned out that he had overdosed on medication. The family could not wake him. An ambulance crew arrived and, an hour later, Shane's death was confirmed.

Eddie D'Alton could relate to the guilt that the families of many suicides experience. He knew his son was a risk of suicide and so he wonders why he did not make sure there were no tablets at home. He also felt let down by the Irish health system and thought the outcome might have been different if Shane had stayed in hospital in Australia. A psychiatrist at the inpatient mental-health facility where Shane was treated explained that there was nothing to indicate that Shane was likely to kill himself. One doctor insisted that given the same circumstances, he would again decide to discharge Shane.

Console, an organisation that assists people bereaved by suicide, helped Eddie cope with the terrible grief, and the questions that arose again and again. He insisted, though, that the emotional burden suicide creates for those left behind was a life sentence. Eddie has started to study counselling so that he might, in the future, be able to help other people in similar situations. He is also determined to spread awareness about depression.

Phyllis McNamara

Phyllis McNamara met her future husband, Michael, when they were both in their mid-teens, but they did not become very close until they studied together at university. What started off as a strong friendship at Trinity College Dublin blossomed into an enduring romance. They married soon after university. Such were the beginnings of a long and wonderful life together. It ended when Michael tragically killed himself in April 2008, after experiencing a spell of self-doubt, anxiety and panic attacks.

Michael had become a solicitor after leaving university and had gone on to develop a very successful practice. Phyllis chronicled the many wonderful things about their life together: shared interests, including cooking, gardening and books; the pride that they both took in their home; and a son who moved to London and enjoyed a successful professional life.

Phyllis was unsure when, exactly, Michael's difficulties began. First, she started to notice him becoming increasingly anxious, which she linked to changed circumstances at work. Michael was uneasy with the fact that he continued to rely on two secretaries, for example, when the younger generation, equipped with ICT skills, typed up most of their own work. Then the stress increased, and he began spending more time in the office than before. He started to worry about some of the financial decisions his clients were taking. After a while, he had difficulties sleeping and started to take sleeping tablets. Phyllis said she was naïve: 'I thought I could fix him with care and love, but I was wrong.'[10]

A holiday to India that Phyllis thought might help Michael's mood did not have the desired effect. Shortly after arriving home, he started to develop panic attacks. Self-doubt plagued him, and he convinced himself that he was no longer competent at work.

In the week before his death, Michael behaved especially bizarrely, Phyllis recalled. He drove either too fast or too slow. His speech was difficult to understand. The evening before he died, Michael admitted to being very frightened, but was unable to explain why. Although Michael had visited a GP and had made an appointment with a psychiatrist, it never entered Phyllis's head that he might kill himself. Yet, the following day, after revealing more self-doubt over supposed mistakes and bad advice he had given clients, that is exactly what Michael did. Phyllis found him hanging from the rafters of their conservatory.

The days and weeks after Michael's death were desperately bleak for Phyllis. She really struggled. Her devastation was such that she seriously contemplated killing herself too. She credited the suicide-prevention and bereavement organisation, Console, with helping her to get through 'those blackest of days.'[11] Pondering the effect that her suicide would have on her son and others close to her was a powerful deterrent against acting on her suicidal impulses.

Phyllis steadfastly believed that we, as a society, need to be able to open up more about the stigmatised subjects of anxiety, depression and mental ill-health, and that because Michael was too ashamed to seek help for his mental-health problem, he took his own life. Phyllis is determined to help tackle such stigmas, and the devastation caused by suicide in Ireland.

Box 6.1 Pieta House

Both John Quinn and Eddie D'Alton recommended that anyone with suicidal feelings contact Pieta House, a suicide- and self-harm-prevention service that offers its services free of charge in eight centres all over Ireland. Named after Michelangelo's sculpture of Mary cradling her dead son, which symbolises compassion, it was set up in 2006 in Dublin by psychologist Joan Freeman, as a place for people with suicidal feelings and their families to go for help. After three years of intensive research into suicide, Freeman says, she came to realise that:

> Most suicides can be prevented and that, in essence, many people are reacting to a life event or a couple of life events and . . . need to be accepted in a loving and compassionate environment and made see that [their difficulties] too will pass and our role isn't to go through their past, our role is to look at their future.[12]

Pieta's compassionate model is non-medical. It focuses on finding solutions to the problems of those who contact the service. The model assumes that suicidal crises can be successfully overcome. It involves nurturing protective factors that will enable people to deal with their current distress, as well as any future crises. Reasons for living are developed, and reasons for dying are tackled. Clients are offered fifteen free therapy sessions, which include elements of two forms of psychotherapy: cognitive behavioural therapy and dialectical behaviour therapy.

Freeman regards Pieta House's services as just one element of the multi-pronged approach that is needed to prevent suicides. She agrees with John Quinn and Eddie D'Alton that people in crisis are referred far too quickly to psychiatric services. She believes that it is usually much more appropriate for someone without a history of mental illness who is experiencing profound distress to avail of services such as Pieta House.

More than 90 percent of Pieta House's funding comes from fundraising. Some 80,000 people participated in its annual fundraising run, called 'Darkness into Light', in May 2014. This kind of support enabled 4,000 people – from children as young as six to people in their eighties – to avail of its services in 2013. It is very close to realising its founder's vision of opening a centre within 100 kilometres of every person in Ireland.

Similarities between suicide stories can be identified. Shane D'Alton and Sean Quinn were both young men who had tried to kill themselves before. They had both promised their families they would not do it again. Like Hemingway, Phyllis McNamara's husband began to experience doubt about his capabilities at work as he grew older. Yet, just as suicide should never be seen as a unitary phenomenon, we must stress that each person who kills themself is unique – and so is their story.

How each family deals with these deaths is also different. Hemingway's wife claimed that his death was a tragic accident, before finally confirming the truth months later. By contrast, Enke's wife chose to speak alongside his doctor at a press conference the day after his death, and tell the world about how her husband had struggled with depression for years.

When we look back after a suicide, we can identify risk factors and life events that make the suicidal outcome appear less surprising. Greater understanding can often be achieved, but we must not err into assuming that any suicide is inevitable. Someone like Hemingway, who had so many risk factors for suicide, was still not bound to die in that way. His previous serious attempts may make it seem that he was intent on ending his life, but his suicide was also the result of the particular circumstances he faced on his last day. If he had been prevented from taking his life on that occasion, there is every reason to believe that he could have avoided a self-inflicted death. Many other people who, like Hemingway, have multiple vulnerabilities choose a different outcome.

At the same time, neither can we assume that these suicides could have been prevented. Different actions may have led to different outcomes in some cases, but it is impossible to establish this definitively. Even people who involve professionals and proactively try to address their vulnerabilities may still kill themselves. Enke sought treatment for his mental illness and kept in regular contact with a psychologist and psychiatrist in the days before his death. He also had access to other resources that should have protected him against death. Just like Michael McNamara, he had good friends and a wife who cared for him deeply. Still, he decided that he could not continue living.

Had these five victims known that their deaths would wreak such devastation amongst those around them, might they have chosen differently? True, Phyllis McNamara's own bereavement experience was central to her decision to resist the suicidal impulse she felt after her husband's death. But our question is in some ways unfair. Many suicidal people are incapable of the rational thought that is required to ponder the effects that their suicide might have on others. We must also acknowledge that, in spite of all we know about these five people, who were all dearly loved, we will never fully understand why they decided to end their lives.

7.
Suicide and the Economy

Modern Greece had never seen anything like it. Seething public anger followed the economic chaos that began there in 2008, and this led to mass demonstrations and violent attacks on financial institutions and other symbols of power.

Though other European countries have experienced turmoil since the unfurling of the financial crisis, none has had to endure as much pain as Greece. Its national debt ballooned from €239 billion to €328 billion between 2007 and 2010, and unemployment soared: more than a quarter of Greeks were jobless in December 2013.[1] For young people, the economic collapse has been catastrophic. In the same month, almost six out of ten young Greeks (58.3 percent) were not working.[2]

The Troika – the International Monetary Fund, the European Commission and the European Central Bank – has since then forced Greece to implement harsh economic remedies. The modern Greek tragedy of austerity has included more than 150,000 enforced job losses in the public sector, reductions in pensions and salaries and huge cuts in public spending.

Greece's health budget has not been spared. It was slashed by almost a quarter between 2009 and 2011. Access to healthcare has been significantly affected. This situation led the World Health Organization to warn Greece and other countries that, 'it should not come as a surprise that we continue to see more stresses, suicides and mental disorders'.[3]

If any country could keep economic woes from driving up its suicide rate, though, surely it would be Greece. As severe as its economic decline has been, suicide has never really been a public-health issue there. When we looked at global suicide rates earlier in this book, we saw that Greece had the lowest one in Europe, with only 3.8 suicide deaths in 2012 for every 100,000 of its people. A Greek is seven times less likely to take his own life than a Lithuanian, for example.

The unavailability of any reliable suicide data as the Greek economic crisis unfolded did not, however, prevent a number of commentators from confidently asserting that this altered economic landscape was leading to a dramatic increase in the number of people taking their own lives. Unofficial data, quoted in Greece's parliament, suggested a 25-percent rise in suicide in 2010 compared to 2009. This turned out to be inaccurate.

However, data on the number of Greeks who killed themselves annually from 2000 through to 2011 is now available and can be scrutinised.

As Figure 7.1 shows, the annual number of suicides has soared by 45 percent between 2007 and 2011, from 328 to 477. That suggests that the economic slump had a large effect on suicide. Looking back at Greek figures during the pre-crisis years, though, shows that suicides declined by 15 percent from 2000 to 2003, dropping from 382 to 323, and then increased by 24 percent from 2003 to 2005, rising to reach 400. Yearly fluctuations in a country's suicide numbers are actually pretty normal and, in a country such as Greece that has a very low base rate, what appear to be large fluctuations are, in fact, random and to be expected.

That said, the increase of more than a hundred suicides (26.5 percent) between 2010 and 2011 is striking. The 477 suicides in 2011 is also a significant deviation from numbers in previous years, and continues the upward trend since the beginning of the crisis. The surge in suicides from 2010 to 2011 was even more startling among women, with twice as many women killing themselves in 2011 (84) than in the previous year (41).

Figure 7.1 | Number of Greek Suicides Annually, 2000-2011

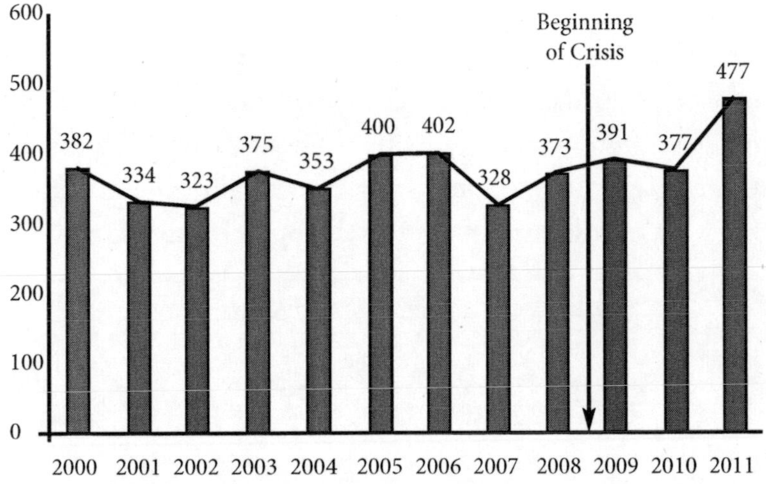

Source: Greek Statistical Authority. www.statistics.gr

There appears then to be a strong association between the recent economic decline and suicide numbers in Greece. This increase is consistent with observations in other countries since the recent economic crisis (more on that later). We say 'appears' because these are observations from what are termed 'ecological data', and it is difficult to reach definitive conclusions following an appraisal of this type of information. All evidence is not created equal, and it helps to have some grasp of the different levels of evidence that emerge from research and data sources when investigating a subject as complex as suicide. We include a brief survey of the different types of evidence in Box 7.1.

Greece is, of course, not the first country in the world to have experienced a severe recession, and the idea that more people kill themselves when an economy is in reverse is not new either. Two of the fathers of the study of suicide – Durkheim and the Italian physician Enrico Morselli – claimed in the nineteenth century that economic difficulties lead to more suicides. Studying historical recessions, then, should help us to explore the accuracy of this view. Durkheim also believed that suicide would increase during rapid economic expansions. Might this also be the case? The most severe recession of the twentieth century, the Great Depression, is a sensible place to start our investigations.

Box 7.1 | The Different Types of Evidence

What makes one piece of evidence more valuable than another? Key considerations are the robustness of the research and the data from which it emerges. This is why organisations such as the WHO and the UK's National Institute for Health and Care Excellence (NICE) rate evidence. The key principles that such organisations use are broadly the same and are illustrated in a rating system developed by the Oxford Centre for Evidence-Based Medicine.[4] Different levels of evidence are assigned to a variety of research studies. The highest level of evidence (1a) is assigned to systematic reviews of randomised controlled trials. The lowest level of evidence (5) is assigned to expert opinion without expert critical appraisal. In between are examples of research types that are more robust than expert opinion but less robust than the gold-standard research methodology that is the randomised controlled trial. Ecological studies (outcomes research) are one example.

Ecological data typically examine the incidence of health conditions or other phenomena in a large population. The suicide data for individual countries that we examined earlier is an example. Ecological studies use such population data to try and identify links between outcomes and a list of possible or suspected causes. Suicide research relies heavily on the findings from ecological data and studies. Though such studies often uncover very strong associations, suggesting that suicide rates decline when alcohol consumption decreases for example, they can never prove that an outcome (suicide) was caused by one factor (decrease in alcohol consumption). Other factors confound the findings – such as mental illness in this example, which influences both alcohol consumption and suicide. The design of these studies also cannot be controlled in the way that a randomised trial can, which facilitates disentangling the individual effects of a factor on an outcome. Often, other confounding factors – perhaps an unknown cultural influence – cannot be identified.

If a finding from an ecological study is replicated in more than one setting, in different countries and cultural contexts, for example, then we can be more confident that the association that has been established is a strong one. Specific types of analysis can also be undertaken on ecological (and other) data to strengthen findings. A meta-analysis is a study that combines the statistical findings from more than one study, thereby increasing the power of the findings of individual studies.

All of this still cannot match the strength of evidence that emerges from randomised controlled trials (RCTs). In simple terms, RCTs are studies in which participants are randomly assigned to different groups after recruitment to a study. All facets of the study should be identical for each group except for the different treatment or intervention they receive. When carried out correctly, any difference in outcomes between the groups at the end of the trial can be said to have been caused by the different interventions. Ideally, we would be able to use RCTs to assess methods used to prevent suicide. Because suicide is such a rare event, however, detecting changes in suicide rates through randomised controlled trials requires several thousand research participants, and the costs of such studies are enormous. So, when answering other suicide questions, we frequently have to make do with less-robust evidence.

The systematic review is a tool that we can avail of when confronted with such situations. It should be a review of all high-quality evidence available on a given topic, but it is also used to arrive at conclusions when lower-quality evidence is available.

Historical Recessions

The Great Depression began in the United States with the stock-market crash of 29 October 1929, known as 'Black Tuesday'. Lasting until 1933, this depression spread from the United States to most other developed economies. An analysis by three researchers – Peter Sainsbury, Jim Jenkins and A. B. Levey – showed that suicides among men between the ages of twenty and thirty-nine increased in fifteen out of twenty countries examined.[5] It also showed that in nineteen of these twenty countries, suicides increased for men between forty and forty-nine. In Finland, suicides among young men increased by 108 percent during the key years. Uncertainty surrounds all associations uncovered in ecological data, so it is possible that self-inflicted deaths may have increased for some reasons other than the economic crisis in each of the individual countries. The Great Depression is, however, the only compelling explanation for why male suicides increased in so many countries.

The link between the Great Depression and increased suicide is also suggested for the United States in a more recent study by Feijun Luo and four colleagues.[6] They reported a 22.8-percent rise in the recorded suicide rate in the USA between 1928 and 1932, which was the largest increase for any four-year period between 1928 and 2007. A major strength of their study was that they extended their investigations to this eighty-year period, during which the US economy experienced many peaks and troughs, and found that the overall suicide rate rose during eleven of thirteen recessions, and fell when the economy was expanding.

Not everybody's fortunes are tied up in equal measure with the ups and downs of the economy. Younger people are more likely to be at school, college or university, and many older people will have retired or may only work part-time. Both groups are, then, less likely to be exposed to the negative effects of an economy in retreat. When the same US analysis focused on suicide rates among different age groups, it found that suicide rates for Americans between the ages of twenty-five and sixty-four increased when the economy shrank but fell when it grew. There were no notable changes to the suicide rates among younger and older groups, though.

So far, it looks like economic decline plays a role in increasing the prevalence of suicide in Western countries – but what about other countries? The most significant economic crisis of the end of the twentieth century happened in Asia between 1997 and 1998. Shu-Sen Chang is a suicide expert based in the University of Hong Kong. Chang and colleagues used a more-robust statistical method, known as time-trend analysis, to examine the link between this particular economic crisis and suicide. Time-trend analysis strengthens findings based on ecological data and tries to identify if there has been a significant deviation from a long-term trend. If a notable change is detected, researchers try to explain why it has occurred by looking at competing explanations.

Chang's analysis identified the number of 'excess' suicides that occurred in 1998, beyond what they would have expected if pre-crisis trends had continued. He and his colleagues found that 10,400 more suicides occurred in Japan, Hong Kong and South Korea in 1998 than would have been expected. There were also especially dramatic increases in male suicide rates in all three countries. Compared to the previous year, they soared by 39 percent in Japan, 44 percent in Hong Kong and 45 percent in South Korea.

The economies of all three countries shrank in 1998. As measured by gross domestic product (GDP), which values all goods and services produced in a country each year, the economy contracted by 2.0 percent in Japan, 5.5 percent in Hong Kong and 6.9 percent in South Korea. Unemployment, which has traditionally been very low in all three economies, increased to 4.1 percent Japan, 4.4 percent in Hong Kong and 7 percent in South Korea.

Economic downturns do not affect all countries equally. In Taiwan and Singapore, which were not hit as severely as their three Asian counterparts, no link between the economic crisis and suicide levels was suggested. The economic slowdown did not prevent Taiwan's economy from growing by 4.5 percent in 1998 and the decline of 1.4 percent in Singapore's GDP in 1998 was smaller than elsewhere. Unemployment also remained below 3 percent in both countries.

Crucially, this suggests that it is the severity of an economic crisis that influences the likelihood of a spike in suicide rates. Considered alongside the historical experience during Western recessions, there are a number of examples which strongly suggest that a rapidly declining economy will be accompanied by a rise in suicides. Cultural factors specific to certain countries and regions will always shape the suicide phenomenon, however. We examine the roles that labour-market conditions and corporate culture play in suicides amongst Japanese professionals in Box 7.2.

Box 7.2 | Suicide Among Working People in Japan

Japan's suicide rate rose dramatically after the Asian economic crisis of 1997 and 1998 and did not stop there. By 2009, more than 30,000 Japanese were killing themselves annually out of a population of 127 million. In most countries, there is generally a higher prevalence of suicide among people in lower-status jobs, the exceptions being people in a few high-status professions like doctors and dentists. When Koji Wada and other academics examined recent mortality in Japan among different occupational groups, however, they found that the greatest increase in the suicide rate since the late 1990s occurred among managers and professional workers.[7] This may be related to a pervasive view in Japan that suicide is an honourable way to die. In 2007, Japan's minister for agriculture, Toshikatsu Matsuoka, became the first cabinet minister to kill himself since the immediate aftermath of the Japanese

---

surrender at the end of the Second World War. He had been accused of corruption and his death by his own hand led one governor to describe him as a 'true samurai'.[8] Those who consider themselves to have failed professionally may be influenced by such powerful cultural beliefs. Koji Wada and his colleagues suggest that increased job demands and more stressful work environments may explain their atypical findings.

Rene Duignan, the Tokyo-based Irish economist we introduced earlier, blames Japanese corporate culture for a large number of Japanese suicides. One manifestation of this is the huge pressure placed on Japanese workers to put in extremely long hours. He cites the Japanese concepts of *honnae* and *tattamae* to help understand what is going on. *Honnae* is a real, tangible thing. *Tattamae* refers to a form of window dressing. In Duignan's words:

> Many companies here in Japan will say – 5.30, go home and enjoy the time with your family and they are the rules but it's only window dressing. There are these unwritten corporate rules that if people leave early, they're selfish and they're leaving the burden on other people and you get then the case that everybody has to stay – it's this kind of peer pressure.[9]

Japanese corporate culture is so ingrained in the fabric of the nation that Duignan is pessimistic about it changing anytime soon. Suicide, unfortunately, appears to be an appealing prospect for many desperate and overworked Japanese professionals.

Why Does Suicide Usually Increase During Recessions?

Unemployment tends to increase dramatically during recessions, and an array of research using different approaches has found an association between unemployment and suicide during economic good times and bad times. This relationship is likely to be confounded by other factors, though. Unemployment is associated with mental illness, for example, which is, in turn, associated with suicide. So it may not be unemployment driving the increase in suicide – at least not directly.

Studies with relatively strong designs, nevertheless, show a strong independent association between unemployment and suicide. Glyn Lewis and Andy Sloggett were able to link English and Welsh census records for 1 percent of the population of England and Wales to mortality records from 1983 to 1992, using what is called a longitudinal approach.[10] This type of study tracks a group of individuals over a sustained period of time and allows us to reach conclusions about the direct effects of statuses such as unemployment.

Lewis and Slogett's study found an independent association between unemployment and suicide and established that unemployed people were 2.6 times more likely to take their own lives than those who had jobs. When they investigated the impacts of most other social and economic factors – such as housing tenure, social class, educational level and access to a car – no relationship was found. Unemployment, then, was the key socio-economic variable driving differences in suicide rates.

During recessions, unemployment increases and those who lose their jobs miss out on the myriad of benefits associated with working, all of which protect against suicide. Having a job is undoubtedly good for your mental health. It provides a structure to our days and can provide many of us with a real sense of purpose. Jobs give status to people and provide opportunities to form friendships and socialise. It is unsurprising, then, that when someone loses a job, it can often be experienced as a traumatic event. The experience may be like bereavement, driving some people over the threshold at which suicide occurs.

Social isolation and mental illness are risk factors for suicide, but unemployment is associated with both. It leaves a person at increased risk of experiencing distress and developing a mental illness such as depression and can also leave him cut off or alienated from mainstream society – as Durkheim insisted happened to people during economic slumps. The availability of less money and resources can make it difficult to meet up with friends.

Men are more likely to be the main breadwinners in their homes, and a move to unemployment that appears to jeopardise their families' futures can seriously erode their self-esteem. This can prompt them to start abusing alcohol or to resort to domestic violence. Some follow through on their suicidal thoughts.

The chief executive of Pieta House, Joan Freeman, says her experience of suicidal men is that many of them are having difficulties adjusting to changed economic circumstances. Whether they have become unemployed or lost a business, she believes they feel they have lost face and a key part of their identity.

The great American journalist, H. L. Mencken, defined a wealthy man as one whose income is $100 higher than his wife's sister's husband. An unemployed man's psychological health may not remain unscathed if he starts unfavourably comparing his current predicament to those around him who are still working.

The research we examined above also highlighted that suicides are more likely to increase when a recession's effects are especially severe. The depth of a recession matters, and so it is likely that distress becomes particularly acute when unemployment persists for longer than might have been expected.

The unemployment that occurs during recessions is not only associated with suicides among the unemployed. Others are also affected. If the unemployed person has a family and children, the changed situation can also increase their risk of suicide, as less household resources can increase the stress on all family members. Even those lucky enough to hold on to their jobs during an economic crisis do not automatically escape the crisis's negative effects. If people around you – at work and in your neighbourhood – are losing their jobs, you may not feel secure. Start worrying that your job might be at risk or that you will not remain immune from the other effects of the recession, and you may well experience deep distress.

As suicide rates are likely to increase during recessions, calls to protect health budgets during recessions appear fairly sensible. It might be expected that our physical health will also suffer during periods of economic crisis. Yet, at least in developed countries, this is surprisingly not the case.

Box 7. 3 | Is a Growing Economy Good for Your Health?

That economic growth is good for your physical health was accepted wisdom in the academic world until the work of Christopher Ruhm suggested the need for a rethink. Ruhm is a former senior economic advisor to US president Bill Clinton. His early work in this area focussed on the United

---

States. He found that the economic growth that the US experienced in the 1970s was linked to more deaths from heart disease.[11] These findings were strengthened when he investigated links between economic conditions and other causes of death in twenty-three developed countries.[12] Ruhm and a colleague found that more people died from heart disease, influenza/pneumonia, liver disease and road-traffic accidents when unemployment fell between 1960 and 1997. Their analysis of the relevant data from the period allowed them to quantify the net effect of unemployment on death. Every 1 percent decrease in the unemployment rate was linked to a 0.4 percent increase in overall deaths. Deaths as a result of motor vehicle accidents rose by 2.1 percent and deaths from liver disease increased by 1.8 percent. Ruhm's broad findings have been confirmed by other researchers elsewhere and suggest a larger effect among men and those of working age.

Investigations using data collected in Sweden for two centuries suggest that economic growth has not always led to increases in overall mortality.[13] Economic progress there in the nineteenth century was associated with better health outcomes, but the situation reversed around halfway through the twentieth century. This suggests that economic development in poorer countries should lead to better health outcomes. It is likely though that a threshold will be reached at a certain stage of economic development, after which decreases in mortality no longer continue.

So what might have changed in richer countries during the twentieth century? Actually, the specific causes of death that Ruhm and co-author Ulf Gerdtham identified as killing more people during periods of economic growth provide some clues. Cardiovascular disease and diseases of the liver are associated with unhealthy behaviours such as drinking alcohol and smoking. When an economy is flourishing and people have more disposable income, they consume more of each. Economic growth can also mean that people work more hours. More time in the office and less time with friends and families can induce stress, which is a known contributor to many illnesses. With less money to go around when an economy stalls, public transport becomes a more popular method of travel. Fewer cars on the road means fewer accidents. Some people will switch to cheaper and healthier alternatives to the car, such as bicycles. Walking also becomes more popular.

The Impact of the Great Recession

Having looked at recent trends in Greece, we argued that a crude examination of the data suggested a strong association between the Great Recession that began in 2008 and increases in the number of people taking their own lives. More robust research carried out using time-trend analysis confirms this link for a number of other countries.

Shu-Sen Chang, an expert on the links between suicide and economic conditions, looked at information collected from fifty-four countries, including Greece, to establish if there was a link between the economic crisis and overall increases in suicide. Chang and his team compared suicide numbers in 2009 with those observed from 2000 to 2007. (So this did not include Greek data for 2010 and 2011, when there was a dramatic spike in suicides there.) They found that there were 4,800 suicides beyond what would have been expected if previous trends had continued.[14] The increases primarily involved men and appeared to be strongly associated with the size of unemployment increases.

Much of the public anger on display since the outbreak of the recent crisis has not been over the economic crisis itself. Instead, demonstrators have targeted most of their rage at the austerity programmes and policies that have been implemented to deal with the recession. We know that recessions are usually associated with more suicides. Yet, how many of these extra deaths are linked to the economic crisis itself, and how many are associated with austerity policies? Chang and his colleagues did not try to answer this and it is, of course, a controversial and politically loaded question. The experiences of other countries during previous recessions may help us to shed some light on the situation.

Can Policy Responses During a Crisis Prevent Suicide?

David Stuckler is a political economist who has written extensively on people's health during recessions. When he finds that a large increase in unemployment is not accompanied by an increase in suicides in a country, he is puzzled.

Take the example of a study that he and four colleagues carried out on links between unemployment and mortality in twenty-six EU countries, from 1970 to 2007.[15] Finland and Sweden stood out, as their suicide rates in the early 1990s behaved differently than the rates in other countries. Suicide rates dropped steadily in Finland between 1990 and 1993, while unemployment soared from 3.2 percent to 16.6 percent. Unemployment in Sweden jumped from 2.1 percent in 1991 to

5.7 percent in 1992 and yet, just as happened in Finland, suicide rates also declined.

Finland and Sweden both had governments committed to providing social support to their citizens, and so the authors speculated that this may have been the reason why the expected increase in deaths from suicide did not happen. They focused particular attention on the role of active labour-market programmes. These played a prominent role in government policies tackling unemployment in both Scandinavian countries. The purpose of such programmes is to improve people's chances of finding work and staying employed. Publicly financed job centres, where unemployed people can find information about vacancies and the provision of employment subsidies, are examples. Most popular in Scandinavian countries, however, have been vocational-training schemes that try to equip unemployed people with skills that will enable them to find work.

Stuckler and his colleagues speculated that these social-support programmes were likely the reason suicide did not increase in either country, but their methods did not allow them to say this conclusively. Competing explanations have also been proposed. Implementation of the world's first national suicide-prevention strategy began in Finland in the early 1990s, and its adherents claim, for example, that this multi-faceted programme was responsible for the reduction in suicides that occurred there.

What Stuckler's findings suggest is that certain policies may act to mitigate the effects of economic decline on suicide. We cannot say for certain whether austerity policies implemented since 2008 are leading to more suicides, independent of the effects of recession. We can be more certain in concluding that Morselli and Durkheim were right to link suicide to the eco-

nomic conditions in society, although Durkheim's view that suicide would also increase during economic booms is not supported by any evidence.

Suicide rates do not go up everywhere every time an economy
goes into reverse. Still, when the evidence from different studies
around the world is weighed up, most of the time, we can expect
– and should be prepared for – more people to take their own
lives when a recession bites. The more severe the recession, the
greater should be our preparedness. This need for vigilance
needs to be tempered by recognition that the causes of suicide
remain complex and multifaceted. As we highlight in the next
chapter, talking up the dangers of suicide, including during a
period of economic retreat, may not in itself be a good thing.

8.
Suicide and the Modern Media: Are We Doing More Harm than Good?

More than two hundred years before Wataru Tsurumi was blamed for causing a surge in suicides in Japan after the publication of his infamous work, *The Complete Manual of Suicide*, the celebrated German writer, Johann Wolfgang von Goethe faced similar accusations. Goethe's novel, *The Sorrows of Young Werther* was released in 1774. It describes the pain and heartache experienced by the novel's protagonist, Werther, because of his affection for the novel's main female character, Charlotte. Charlotte eventually marries Albert, who happens to be a friend of Werther's. Unable to cope with the situation, Werther decides that one of them must die and ends up shooting himself with Albert's pistol.

It was widely believed at the time that Goethe's work led to a wave of young men deciding to end their lives all over Europe. Some men who killed themselves were discovered dressed in the same manner as Goethe's descriptions of Werther. Others used a similar pistol. Copies of the novel were even found beside a number of suicide victims. The damning evidence that Goethe's novel was responsible, in the eyes of many of his contemporaries, was the fact that the copies found at the scenes of these deaths were frequently open to the page at which the suicide occurs. The novel was subsequently banned in a number of European states. Goethe included an anti-suicide warning in later editions.

The suicide researcher David Phillips invented the term 'the Werther effect' to refer to the phenomenon through which a well-publicised suicide leads to copycat suicides. Yet, does the Werther effect really exist? And, if so, what media formats influence suicidal behaviour? If media coverage leads to copycat suicides, might it also be possible for certain media coverage to protect against suicides? We will look at modern portrayals of actual and fictional suicides and suicidal behaviour to try to answer these questions.

Coverage of Actual Suicides

Newspapers and television dominate the modern media's coverage of suicides. Both show a particular interest in suicide stories concerning celebrities. Estonians Merike Sisask and Airi Värnik have carried out the most comprehensive review, investigating the impact of the reporting of suicide on suicidal behaviour.[1] We can conclude from their findings that such reporting confirms the reality of the Werther effect. Of the fifty-six studies they examined, fifty-two showed that media coverage of suicide leads to more suicidality, i.e. a mix of more suicide fatalities, more attempts and greater suicidal ideation.

Some of the most potent effects follow an editorial decision to cover a celebrity suicide. In such a case, copycat effects are more likely among those of the same gender and age as the superstar.

Women in their thirties were, then, more at risk of suicide after Marilyn Monroe's death in 1962 was widely publicised. Leslie Cheung, Eun-ju Lee and Min-Jan Nee were not household names in the West, but they were all famous in their home countries when they ended their lives between 2003 and 2005.

Cheung was a celebrated singer and actor who received eight best-actor nominations at the Hong Kong Film Awards. He was also a gay icon after he became one of the few Chinese celebrities to reveal that he was homosexual. On 1 April 2003, while Hong Kong was in the midst of an outbreak of SARS, Cheung jumped to his death from the Mandarin Oriental Hotel. He left behind a suicide note that revealed he had been battling depression.

Eun-ju Lee was a South Korean actress who killed herself in February 2005. Her family linked her death to emotional struggles, insomnia and depression. Her decision to take part in sex scenes in her final film, the *Scarlet Letter* was said to have been the source of much of her distress. Min-Jan Nee was a Taiwanese actor and comedian who took his own life in April 2005, shortly after it was alleged that he had been having an affair with a well-known actress.

Suicide experts King-wa Fu and Paul Yip examined the impacts of the deaths of all three of these celebrities on suicides in each of their home countries.[2] Their research made use of a time-series analysis. Similar to studies we featured in our survey of the impact of economic downturns on suicide, Fu and Yip were able to compare deaths in the weeks after the suicides with a reference period. They chose the two years prior to the suicides. They combined data from three different countries (a meta-analysis), which further strengthened their findings.

They found that there was a substantial rise in the number of suicides in the first, second and third weeks after the death of each celebrity in Hong Kong, South Korea and Taiwan. When the information on fatalities in all three countries was combined, it showed that there was a 40-percent increase in risk among people of the same gender as the celebrities in the first four weeks after the suicides, compared to the reference period. Fu and Yip also grouped all of the deaths from suicide into four different age categories, so that they could compare the ages of the fatalities to those of the deceased celebrity. They found that the risk of suicide among people in the same age category as the famous suicide increased by half (49 percent) in the four weeks after their deaths. The increased risk for people of the same gender who were also in the same age bracket was 56 percent in the same four-week period.

You did not have to be a fan of Leslie Cheung's music or his films. Merely by being a male in your late forties who lived in Hong Kong at the time of his death (and hearing about it), your risk of suicide increased by more than half in the month after he died.

Experience in Asia has also shown how the reporting of a novel suicide method in the mainstream media is linked to its increased use in many subsequent suicides. In 1980, the deaths of two girls in Sri Lanka who had deliberately consumed the poisonous seeds of the yellow oleander shrub were widely reported. This reporting appears to have been linked to a notable increase in the popularity of such poisoning. Jaffna Hospital, in the north of the country, recorded no admissions related to oleander poisoning in 1979 but admitted 103 cases in 1983.

The first known case of suicide in Hong Kong by charcoal burning involved a middle-aged woman in 1998 and was prominently featured the territory's local media. At the end of that year, suicide by charcoal burning accounted for less than 2 percent of suicides in Hong Kong. Its surge in popularity meant that by 1999, one in ten people taking their lives in the territory chose to do so by burning charcoal in a closed room to asphyxiate themself. Two years later, charcoal burning accounted for around a quarter of all suicides. The dramatic increase in suicide by this new method was not accompanied by a decline in the popularity of other methods, so there was a 20-percent rise in the overall suicide rate.

The media today continue to advertise dramatic and highly lethal methods used in suicides.[3] In addition to charcoal burning, these include shooting, jumping and railway and subway suicides. Such methods are not at all representative of how people actually end their lives. Worldwide, hanging and pesticide poisoning continue to dominate as methods. One potential danger of media coverage of atypical methods is that it can lead people to switch from less-lethal suicide methods to more-deadly ones.

David Phillips's research findings from the 1970s caution against placing stories about suicide on the front pages of newspapers. He showed that there was an increase in the number of suicides following the coverage of suicides on the front pages of newspapers.[4] The front-page coverage given to the death of Marilyn Monroe in the *New York Times* was associated with an increase of approximately 2 to 3 percent in the national suicide rate in the United States some seven to ten days after the story appeared.

Why Does Suicidal Behaviour Increase After Media Reporting?

The media is, of course, one of the most important sources of information and learning. Social learning theory assumes we are all likely to imitate behaviours learned from others. Troubled and vulnerable people who become aware of suicide as an option are much more likely to copy such behaviour, however, especially when the media romanticises suicide – or presents it as the logical result of particular difficulties. Negative portrayals, on the other hand, can indicate that suicide is wrong or focus on the devastation experienced by loved ones in the aftermath of such a fatality. The theory assumes that such negative representations should make copycat suicides less likely.

Social learning of suicidal behaviours can be especially powerful when vulnerable people 'vertically' identify with others that they admire, such as celebrities. They may reason that if a famous person decides to end his life, this is a normal reaction to life's difficulties, and so they are justified in taking similar action too. Children who imitate parental suicidal behaviours can do so as a result of a similar learning process.

A different perspective, dose-response theory, simply proposes that the greater the amount and prominence of coverage given to a suicide, the greater the copycat effects will be. Front-page coverage, headline coverage and copious amounts of articles are especially dangerous, then. The suicide stories of Leslie Cheung, Min-Jan Nee and Eun-ju Lee were all covered in this way.

We can find support for both social learning theory and dose-response theory, although social learning theory's assumption that negative definitions can curtail suicide is questionable.

Fictional Portrayals of Suicide in TV and Film

Television and film have long overtaken the novel as the most common media formats in which fictional events are portrayed. Stanley Kubrick's *Full Metal Jacket*, four film versions of Romeo and Juliet (see below) and Frank Darabont's *The Shawshank Redemption* all include dramatic suicides. Television dramas and soap operas create the potential for viewers to witness suicidal behaviour in characters that they have become familiar with over the course of months and years. Australian Jane Pirkis and a number of research colleagues were unable to offer conclusive answers to questions surrounding the impact of fictional suicides on actual suicidal outcomes in the general population.[5]

This is best illustrated by the results of five studies that assessed how broadcasting an episode of the British soap *EastEnders* on 2 March 1986 affected suicidal behaviour in the population at large. The episode involved an attempted overdose by Angie, a character in her thirties. All of the studies assessed attendance at accident-and-emergency departments in the UK before and after the episode.

The first relevant study concentrated on Hackney Hospital in London.[6] Authors Simon Ellis and Susan Walsh compared overdose presentations in the week after the episode with the average number of presentations in the ten weeks before the episode. Comparisons were extended to also include the average number of presentations in the same week during the previous ten years. This showed that there was an increase in the number of relevant presentations in the week following the episode. Two subsequent studies made some slight changes to Ellis and Walsh's methodology and focused their investigations on other parts of the UK. They also found that the episode led to copycat suicidal behaviour.[7,8]

We might conclude so far that the appearance of Angie's overdose on television undoubtedly had negative repercussions. For solid scientific reasons, researchers want to see findings replicated, and they regularly change methodologies to assess the robustness of various conclusions. This was the case with two subsequent research papers that examined the same broadcast.

The first made some changes to the methodology used by Ellis and Walsh. Overdose presentations in London's St Bartholomew's Hospital were added to the study, along with those in Hackney Hospital. Different time frames were also selected. This investigation compared the number of overdose presentations during the two weeks before and after the episode with the number in corresponding periods in two previous years. This time, the episode was found not to have had any impact. Although there was an increase in the number of self-poisoning presentations after the airing of the *EastEnders* episode, an increase in suicide attempts had actually began before the broadcast.[9] A fifth study reported mixed findings. Results showed there was an increase in overdose presentations by women but not in the overall number of presentations.[10]

The inconclusive findings on the impact of this episode mirror the overall findings of Pirkis's review. Some studies provided evidence for a copycat effect, but some did not. Mixed findings were reported in others. We just cannot be sure, then, whether fictional portrayals of suicidal behaviour on film and television increase its incidence in the population.

Box 8.1 Portrayals of Romeo and Juliet on Film

Probably the best-known fictional representation of suicide takes place in *Romeo and Juliet*, Shakespeare's play about two young lovers from feuding families in Verona. The besotted couple marry the day after their first meeting. Juliet, meanwhile, takes a drug that sends her into a temporary sleep in an

---

attempt to avoid marrying her family's chosen suitor. Her family are convinced she is actually dead, as is a grief-stricken Romeo, who then kills himself by drinking poison. Waking from the effects of the drug and discovering a dead Romeo, Juliet ends her life by stabbing herself with her lover's dagger.

Patrick Jamieson explored how suicide was portrayed in four different film versions of Shakespeare's classic, which were released in 1936, 1954, 1969 and 1996.[11] He found that the ages of the lead actors fell considerably from George Cukor's 1936 adaptation, which starred Leslie Howard (forty-four) and Norma Shearer (thirty-four), to Renato Castellani's 1954 version with Laurence Harvey (twenty-six) and Susan Shentall (twenty). It decreased again in 1969, when Olivia Hussey (seventeen) and Leonard Whiting (eighteen) played the leading roles in Franco Zeffirelli's film. Leonardo DiCaprio (twenty-two) was a little older when he played the lead with Claire Danes (seventeen) in Baz Luhrmann's 1996 version. The preference of directors for younger actors reflects the media's fascination with suicide among younger people and a general disinterest in stories of suicide involving older people, who are usually much more likely to end their lives.

More time was devoted to the acts of suicide in the two more-recent releases than in Castellani's 1954 version. Juliet's suicide got a complete Hollywood makeover in 1996, when she used a gun to kill herself. The three earlier versions showed her ending her life with a dagger. All of the films deviated significantly from Shakespeare's text, by offering a positive definition of suicide. Viewers were led to believe that the couple would be re-united in the afterlife.

Irresponsible and Responsible Media Reporting of Suicide

On 6 August 1962, the day after Marilyn Monroe's death, the *New York Times* led with the headline MARILYN MONROE DIES – PILLS NEAR. The story's second paragraph said an empty bottle of sleeping pills was found beside her bed and fourteen other bottles of medicine were on her night stand. Contemporary wisdom stresses that newspapers should never refer, as the *Times* did, to the methods used by people to kill themselves.

Nevertheless, the irresponsible reporting of suicide in certain media outlets continues. The Taiwanese media's coverage of the death of comedian Min-Jan Nee was in particularly bad taste. After his death, footage of the tree from which he had hung himself was regularly aired. His wife and children were pursued by journalists, who targeted them with insensitive questions. The woman with whom Nee was alleged to have been having an affair did not escape the paparazzi's attention either.

Coverage of the deaths of Nee, Leslie Cheung and Eun-ju Lee ignored a number of the WHO media guidelines for preventing suicide.[12] Developed in response to what we know about the potential negative effects of the media on suicide rates, they advise against including prominent front-page coverage of suicide fatalities, photographs or information on the personal backgrounds of those who have died. In the case of Leslie Cheung, Min-Jan Nee and Eun-ju Lee, all of the above advice was ignored by multiple journalists.

More recently, the *New York Daily News*'s 13 August 2014 front-page story on Robin Williams's death showed contempt for these key guidelines. Its prominent headline, HANGED, was accompanied by a gaunt picture of Williams and a number of subheadings that provided more information on his death. Lest the reader be in any doubt that Williams had actually hung himself, the tabloid's subheadings confirmed that he had tied a belt around his neck. Readers were also informed that he had slashed one of his wrists with a penknife.

The WHO promotes eleven media guidelines on suicide. They are based on the assumption that just as there is potential for the media to have harmful effects, it can also play a protective role. The reduction of the suicide rate by media content is known as the 'Papageno effect', which takes its name from the character Papageno in Mozart's opera *The Magic Flute*. He tries to hang himself after convincing himself that he will never win over his love, Papagena. He is persuaded by three child-spirits, however, not to end his life and to beckon Papagena with his magic bells. *The Magic Flute* has a happier ending for Papageno than Goethe's *Werther*. The couple are happily reunited before the end of the opera.

Those who advocate a protective role for the media can point to the example offered by Vienna's experience in the 1980s with subway suicides. Concerns over the role that media publicity may have played in such fatalities led the Austrian Association for Suicide Prevention, Crisis Intervention and Conflict Resolution in 1987 to develop some of the earliest media guidelines. Crucially, the city's main newspapers decided to substantially curtail the publicity that had previously surrounded these deaths; by July of 1987, such deaths were no longer mentioned. There was a progressive fall in the number of subway suicides and attempts involving this method. Fatalities fell from fourteen in 1986 to just four in 1990, and there was no corresponding increase in the number of self-inflicted deaths by other methods. The number of subway suicides remained low for the subsequent five years.

The chronology of events certainly suggests that the introduction of the media guidelines led to fewer suicides. A more objective assessment, however, must conclude that we just do not know if this is the case. The small number of suicides involved, in particular, means that caution needs to be exercised in inferring too much from the Viennese experience.

Media guidelines that promote responsible reporting on suicide encourage journalists to focus on the quality of their stories, avoiding sensational reporting, as well as the quantity, reducing the amount of coverage. However, after completing a study that focussed on teenage suicide rates and finding that none of the quality characteristics of stories affected rates, David Phillips and a number of colleagues concluded that issues of quality are far less relevant.[13] Another expert in the area, Robert Goldney, has also shown that the neutral reporting of suicide can prompt vulnerable people to kill themselves.[14] The logical conclusion is that ceasing reporting on suicide altogether could reduce suicide rates significantly. The power of the Internet and the spread of social media, however, mean that this may be impossible.

Box 8.2 | The Dangers Posed by the Internet and New Media

Bullying has longed been linked to distress and, on occasion, suicidal behaviour, especially among adolescents. The spread of social media means that a new type of bullying has emerged. Such cyberbullying was linked to a number of high-profile suicides in Ireland in 2012, including those of three teenagers and a prominent politician. Shane McEntee, a minister of state, had been the subject of savage online criticism

---

following his robust defence of government policies. At his funeral, his brother directed his anger at these bullies:

'Shame on you people, you faceless cowards who sent him horrible messages'.[15]

A further threatening development made possible by modern media is the ability of anyone to publish uncensored material online. A particular danger is pro-suicide content written by those who present suicide as a solution and urge people to end their lives. Some distressed individuals are also making suicide pacts with people they have never met.

The development of social media and the increasing accessibility of the Internet mean that vulnerable people can now get news about suicide and information on how they might kill themselves much more easily than ever. Less than twenty-four hours after actor Robin Williams ended his life, there would not have been too many people with Internet connections who did not know that his death was a suspected suicide.

The copycat-suicide phenomenon that the elders of Miletus tackled by publicly displaying the naked bodies of female suicide victims continues to trouble us. What did not exist in ancient Greece was media that rapidly spread the news of celebrity suicides. Expecting the mainstream media to cease covering suicides altogether, however, is hopelessly unrealistic. Journalists and editors will maintain that the public has an interest in knowing how people such as Robert Enke and L'Wren Scott died. The surge in the coverage of suicides in the media, on film and on television, largely reflects public concern and interest in the issue.

German media covered Robert Enke's suicide responsibly and sympathetically. His wife took the brave decision to publicly reveal, the day after his death, his long struggles. German chancellor Angela Merkel reflected the compassionate mood of the country's journalists and the public when she revealed that she had written a very personal letter to Teresa Enke. All the same, German rail reported a spike in the number of people ending their lives by leaping in front of trains in the weeks after his death. Guidelines promoting the responsible reporting of suicides, therefore, may have only limited effects.

We must also question whether other media coverage on the topic of suicide is of any benefit. Might the Irish media's obsession with the numbers of young people taking their lives and their suggestions for tackling this problem actually be damaging? World Suicide-Prevention Day takes place every September and consumes a number of column inches in Irish national and regional newspapers. Readers may learn about the work of a suicide-prevention agency or a crisis service and the motivated and dedicated people who work there. Staff include professionals and volunteers, many of whom have themselves been bereaved by suicide. Articles often have an educational component, informing readers about common symptoms of depression and sources of help available to someone who feels suicidal. Such media coverage can also be found during most other weeks of the year. Can we be certain, though, that such sympathetic coverage is not leading more people to kill themselves?

Such coverage has undoubtedly helped to generate awareness of the problem, and yet studies evaluating the impact of public-information campaigns that relate to suicide have been unable to find any evidence that they reduce deaths. More people are now talking about suicide than ever before, but the assumption that this must be a good thing may be misguided. There is no evidence that sympathetic references to suicide are damaging. It is very likely, however, that references on the radio, television, online and in the print media mean that more and more vulnerable people are at risk of seeing suicide as a legitimate response to stressful circumstances.

9.
The Rights and Wrongs
of Suicide

In April 2002, an Irish government minister and general practitioner, Dr Jim McDaid, said people who take their own lives are 'selfish bastards'.[1] McDaid insisted that he wanted to encourage young people to reflect on the effects of suicide on others. After a torrent of criticism, he apologised and withdrew his comments. Dr John Connolly reflected much of this criticism when he insisted that, 'there is still a considerable amount of stigma attached to suicide and these statements are quite hurtful. It's like saying that people who are ill are selfish bastards. Nobody chooses to be ill.'[2]

Some of the other accusations thrown at McDaid were that his remarks revealed him to be cruel and insensitive. But was such criticism misdirected? Should we, in fact, sometimes describe those who die by suicide or who attempt to end their lives as cruel and insensitive? Radical priest John Eldrid, former chair of the Samaritans in the UK, has written that:

> the person who commits suicide puts his psychological skeletons in the survivor's emotional closets – he sentences the survivors to deal with many negative feelings, and, more, to become obsessed with thoughts regarding their own actual or

possible role in having precipitated the suicidal act or having failed to abort it. It can be a heavy load.[3]

Eldrid certainly implied that some people who take their lives are selfish because they display insufficient regard for the impacts of their suicides on those left behind. But can we pass an ethical or moral judgment on those who kill themselves? The assumed link between suicide and mental illness means that debates about the rights and wrongs of suicide have often been seen as pointless or even inappropriate. Suicide, it is asserted, can never be judged in the same way as other acts, because the person who takes their own life is ill and they are a victim.

Rene Duignan highlights some very real dangers of even debating the morality of suicide. When he speaks on suicide prevention in Japan, he is regularly asked about justifiable suicides. He believes these questions are often posed by people thinking about killing themselves. Understandably reluctant to condone suicide in the presence of a vulnerable person, he takes a very strong line that suicide is never justifiable.[4] Notwithstanding Duignan's views, many other commentators believe that the morality of suicide is a very important topic worth discussing, and that it is open to interpretation. Just because suicide – or any other act – should be prevented, that does not necessarily make it wrong.

Is Suicide Wrong?

Making a moral judgement on suicide is far from a simple task and ultimately depends on one's perspective on the world. Our earlier exploration of the history of suicide revealed how taking one's own life could be approved of or condemned in the societies of ancient Rome and Greece. Influential philosophers have taken different views on the subject. The Stoic school of philosophy, which was influential in ancient Greece and Rome, maintained, for instance, that suicide at the right time and for the right reasons was a good thing.

Ever since Christianity became a dominant force in Western society, important thinkers have pronounced on the rights and wrongs of suicide. Those lining up to support a right to suicide, like the Stoics, have included the Renaissance humanist Erasmus of Amsterdam, the French Enlightenment political thinker Montesquieu, the Scottish philosopher David Hume, and the eighteenth-century writers Voltaire and Goethe.

Joining Augustine of Hippo and the thirteenth-century theologian Thomas Aquinas in disapproving of suicide was the eighteenth-century German philosopher Immanuel Kant. More recently, Ludwig Wittgenstein, who taught philosophy at the University of Cambridge in the first half of the twentieth century and lost three of his brothers to suicide, emerged as a powerful opponent of a right to suicide.

Augustine affirmed that all suicides are wrong, based on the biblical prohibition outlined in the fifth commandment. The instruction 'Thou shalt not kill' reflects a sacred principle that killing is fundamentally wrong and is used by many contemporary Catholics and religious conservatives to insist that murder, abortion, euthanasia and suicide are all wrong.

Kant saw suicide as always wrong because it deviated from his view of the ideal person as a rational agent with autonomy of will. Using that will to destroy the body that otherwise puts our wishes into action was, he believed, a complete contradiction and an affront to the unique moral nature of humanity. The true test of the morality of an action could be determined by considering what would happen if everyone carried it out. Would it help or hinder society? As the universal application of suicide would lead to the end of all human life, he insisted that it could not be supported.

In contrast, utilitarians such as the English philosopher and political economist John Stuart Mill believed that the morality of an individual action was ultimately determined by its consequences. Acts that produce the greatest happiness for the greatest number of people should be approved of. So, in Mill's framework, suicide could be right or wrong depending on the outcome. His classical liberal perspective holds that each individual has the right to act as they want, subject only to the harm principle, which constrains any individual actions that cause harm to others. If the wife and children of someone who takes his life are left destitute following his death, we should not approve of the suicide. Academic Donald H. Regan cites the example of the soldier who kills himself to protect secret military information as a suicide that would be approved of by utilitarian ethics.[10] Clearly, the consequences of him staying alive are very likely to be torture and the betrayal of key information, which would lead to much worse damage for his colleagues and his cause. There is not an obligation on him to kill himself, but there are legitimate reasons why he may take such a decision.

Might there be an alternative position, then, to Augustine's and Kant's strict prohibitions? An alternative position that considers the circumstances of different cases of suicide before arriving at an ethical judgment? Is suicide really always wrong?

Consider the case of a person with a deteriorating terminal illness who experiences constant pain and suffering. Let us ignore assisted suicide for the moment and try to establish first if this person might have a right to kill themself. We are assuming that they have the physical capacity to do so and therefore do not need to rely on others. On what might they base a right to kill themself? We construe this debate as Utah-based ethics professor Margaret 'Peggy' Battin has done: as one between competing moral principles.

Usually, two basic principles or human rights, which are widely accepted in liberal democratic Western societies, can be advanced in favour of the right of a terminally ill person to kill themself: the right to autonomy or liberty and the right to mercy. Autonomy means that we get to decide as much about our lives as possible, subject only to the harm constraint. Imagine if someone else got to decide who your friends were, who you must marry or which football team you must support. Most of us would doubtless object strongly. And, as liberty extends to all aspects of our lives, it should also apply to the ends of our lives and how we choose to die.

What about the possibility that suicide in this situation does cause harm to others? The suicide of a loved one, even one who is terminally ill, may still impact relatives and friends negatively. Still, is the creation of the psychological skeletons that Eldrid identified inevitable? Surely, a reasoned discussion with loved ones should greatly assist the acceptance of such a decision – although it cannot guarantee acceptance. While attempts to minimise any harm to others must be undertaken, it is still unreasonable to expect that a person who is suffering must be forced to continue living to satisfy the wishes of others.

A person with a terminal illness, by killing themself, is also exercising a right to forego needless pain and suffering. Despite advances in modern medicine and palliative care, all pain and suffering cannot always be eliminated, and suicide quite clearly ensures it will be. Mercy dictates that a person has a right to suicide in such a situation. The only logical reason for denying them this right in such circumstances is if we can unearth other principles of equal or greater weight than autonomy and mercy.

Oppose the right of the terminally ill person to kill themself and you will likely point out that killing anyone, including yourself, is fundamentally wrong. This principle of the intrinsic wrongness of killing may be of equal or greater weight than the rights of autonomy and mercy. Deviations from it are, nonetheless, commonplace. Most of us accept, for instance, that killing in self-defence or during a just war is justified.

We conclude that a terminally person who is experiencing intolerable pain and suffering has the right to kill themself, and so, take a different position than Augustine and Kant. Therefore, all suicides are not wrong. This, then, leads to the question of whether helping someone kill themself is always wrong.

Euthanasia and Assisted Suicide

Several governments in North America and Europe have legalised euthanasia and assisted suicide. The US state of Oregon passed the Death with Dignity Act in 1997, which legalised physician-assisted suicide. The US states of Washington, Montana, Vermont and New Mexico have since followed suit. Switzerland was the first country in the world to legalise physician-assisted suicide, in 1942. It would be sixty years before another country legalised the practice. Voluntary euthanasia and assisted suicide have both been legal in the Netherlands since 2002. In February 2014, the Belgian parliament controversially lifted all age restrictions on euthanasia, allowing terminally ill children to choose to die. What some label as 'suicide tourism' is also on the rise. More than 600 non-residents from thirty-one countries travelled to Switzerland to avail of an assisted suicide between 2008 and 2012.[5]

Euthanasia and assisted suicide must be distinguished from other cases of suicide, as they do not meet Durkheim's definition as arising from an act of the dead person himself. Philosopher and author Jennifer Hecht refers to this type of death not as suicide but as 'end-of-life management'.[6] Here, death is seen as fairly imminent anyway, and it can be argued that people are not taking their own lives but rather changing the manner in which their illness kills them. In the US state of Washington, the terminally ill person who wants to die must be able to self-administer the medication that will kill them, which has been prescribed by a doctor. This is not legally classified as suicide. The terminal illness is listed as the cause of death.

Having prompted debates around the world about how we should and should not die, assisted suicide and euthanasia cannot be ignored. They are highly relevant.

Box 9.1 | Definitions

- Suicide: Death resulting directly or indirectly from a positive or negative act of the victim, which the victim knows will produce this result.[7]

- Euthanasia: The painless killing of a patient suffering from an incurable and painful disease or in an irreversible coma.[8]

- Assisted Suicide: The suicide of a patient suffering from an incurable disease, effected by the taking of lethal drugs provided by a doctor for this purpose.[9]

Assisted Suicide

Commonly, as in the case of Marie Fleming (see Box 9.2), the right of a terminally ill person to end their life focuses on the right to an assisted suicide. Many terminally ill people who want to die are also so incapacitated by their illness that they are no longer physically able to kill themselves and may also want a more dignified and painless way of dying than is associated with many of the more common methods of suicide.

In the ethical debate over the right to assisted suicide, the rights to autonomy and mercy are, again, relevant considerations. Realising your rights of autonomy and mercy, though, now require that someone else helps you to die – usually a doctor. The crucial difference in this debate is that those who oppose a right

---

Box 9.2 | Marie Fleming's Fight for the Right to Die

The plight of Marie Fleming attracted international attention in 2012 and 2013, when she brought a case before Ireland's courts, seeking the right to die. She had developed multiple sclerosis in 1989, while in her mid-thirties, and the progressive nature of the disease meant that twenty years later she required full-time care and was in constant pain. She could not use her arms or legs, had no control over her bladder and had difficulty swallowing liquids. Five years previously, she had considered travelling to Switzerland, where she would have been able to avail of its assisted-dying laws. Much more gravely ill in 2012, however, Marie Fleming could no longer travel abroad and was incapable of killing herself.

Though Ireland's Criminal Law (Suicide) Act had decriminalised suicide in 1993, it introduced a penalty of up to fourteen years in prison for any person who helps someone kill

---

themself. Fleming was seeking an assurance that her partner and full-time carer, Tom Curran, would not be prosecuted if he helped her. She argued that Ireland's ban on assisted suicide was incompatible with European human-rights norms and that Ireland's Constitution granted her the right to die. She also maintained that Irish law discriminated against her on the grounds of her disability because, unlike an able-bodied person, she was unable to kill herself and required the assistance of another person. Her evidence so moved the President of the High Court, Mr Justice Nicholas Kearns, that he described her as, 'in many ways the most remarkable witness which any member of this court has ever been privileged to encounter'.[10]

Margaret 'Peggy' Battin testified on behalf of Fleming by video link. Battin's lifelong interest in end-of-life care was sparked by her mother's difficult death from liver cancer when Peggy was only twenty-one. She is a passionate believer in the right of terminally ill people who suffer to have access to assisted suicide. A tragic accident in 2008 that left her husband paralysed from the shoulders down did give cause for second thoughts, but her beliefs have not diminished. Though Battin assured the court that there is no evidence from those countries where it has been introduced that legalising assisted suicide has a disproportionate impact on vulnerable groups, the court found that:

> it would be impossible to ensure that the aged, the disabled, the poor, the unwanted, the rejected, the lonely, the impulsive, the financially compromised would not avail of this option to avoid a sense of being a burden on their family and society.[11]

Fleming shook her head when Kearns uttered these words. The other grounds for her case were also dismissed.

Undeterred, Fleming appealed her case to Ireland's highest court, the Supreme Court, which rejected her appeal in April 2013. That court found that no explicit right to die was contained in the Irish Constitution, and one could not be deduced from other rights. The right to life did not, for instance, convey a right to die, because the court held that such a right was the complete opposite of the social order contemplated by the values reflected in the Constitution. Although Ireland was found not to be in breach of European human-rights norms, like other states, it was free to introduce legislation to deal with divisive issues such as assisted suicide.

Fleming eventually succumbed to the effects of her illness, dying in December 2013. Her partner, Curran, continues the fight for others to have the right that was denied Fleming. He is working with legal experts to draft an assisted-dying bill to be introduced to Ireland's parliament.

to assisted suicide can introduce another argument alongside the belief that killing is fundamentally wrong.

They can use a 'slippery slope' argument, maintaining that if our society sets a precedent that allows assisted suicide in a limited number of circumstances, it will launch us towards also allowing people to die in cases when it is entirely inappropriate. Soon, deceitful family members will be able to kill their frail relatives or these same relatives may feel pressurised to choose to die because of the financial burden that their medical care is imposing on their families. It is also claimed that vulnerable groups such as people with disabilities will be killed against their wishes.

As Peggy Battin points out, the main difficulty with this argument is its claim that change must not be made to current arrangements because of the risk that it *might* lead to a greater evil. There are, of course, a range of other possible outcomes that could result from relaxing laws on suicide. To disallow change because of the possibility of one such outcome is unreasonable.

Safeguards against potential abuse can, moreover, be introduced. The Oregon Death with Dignity Act requires that a patient requesting physician-assisted suicide must have been diagnosed with a terminal illness and have less than six months to live. Two doctors must confirm this prognosis. The person must also have their request witnessed by two people. Neither witness can be a relative, be entitled to any portion of the person's estate or work for any health-care facility caring for the person. If mental incapacity, mental illness or depression is suspected, a psychiatric or psychological evaluation must also take place. Assisted suicides in Oregon account for only 0.2 percent of all deaths, and even where much-more-liberal legislation exists, in the Netherlands, voluntary euthanasia and assisted suicide account for less than 3 percent of total deaths.

The conclusions of Ireland's High Court in Marie Fleming's case ignored the evidence from Oregon and the Netherlands that safeguards have ensured that the concerns aired in 'slippery slope' arguments are unfounded. Three Dutch government studies on end-of-life decisions from 1990 have shown that there is no evidence that any pressure was placed on vulnerable people or that anyone was forced to die against their wishes.[12] The slippery slope argument, then, does not overturn the moral right to assisted suicide in such circumstances.

Box 9.3 | To Censor or Not to Censor? Is It Right to Produce a Suicide Manual?

Derek Humphry's wife was dying from inoperable cancer and in 1975, she asked her husband to help her to die. After witnessing her struggles with the pain caused by the cancer, he agreed. Humphry has been a passionate advocate for the acceptance of rational suicide for the terminally ill ever since.

Still, Humphry stunned even many of those who sympathised with his liberal convictions when he published his guide to self-deliverance, *Final Exit* in 1991. At the beginning of the book, Humphry asks those contemplating ending their lives because of depression or because they cannot cope not to use his book. He pleads with readers to 'respect the true intentions of *Final Exit*: the right of a terminally ill person with unbearable suffering to know how to choose to die'.[13]

In *Final Exit*, Humphry reviews several methods by which terminally ill people can end their lives. He discusses the pros and cons of each before recommending a preferred method: asphyxiation using a plastic bag. Later editions of the book change the recommendation to inhaling helium using a bag or helium hood. Humphry then provides detailed instructions as to how a person can go about killing himself using his recommended method.

Even Humphry knew that there was a strong likelihood that the information he presented was likely to be misused. Some of the fears of those condemning the publication of his book were apparently immediately realised. A study showed that suicide by asphyxiation increased by more than 300 percent in New York City in the year after *Final Exit*'s publication.[14] And just as had sometimes happened with Goethe's novel about young Werther, copies of Humphry's book were found at the sites of a quarter of suicides by asphyxiation in New York City in 1992. This study could not show that the overall suicide rate had increased in New York City or that persons who did not have a terminal illness had used this method. Humphry, himself, claimed that the effect of his book was merely to change the method by which some people ended their lives.

Final Exit remains banned in France. Bookshops and university libraries elsewhere have taken the decision not to stock it, and yet it has still sold over one million copies worldwide. Should it be freely available? Are we irresponsible to even identify this book? If harm to others should curtail a right to liberty, then a strong case can be made that books such as *Final Exit* should not be available.

How Should We Judge Suicide?

By finding that suicide and assisted suicide are justified in some circumstances, we do not propose to argue that suicide is always right. As an extreme example, the tactical use of suicide to kill civilians through the use of suicide bombings can never be justified. It is plainly wrong. It is also, of course, an atypical suicide, because the bomber is not only aiming to kill themself, but also to kill as many bystanders as possible. Such a suicide fails our morality test by destructively and deliberately seeking to harm innocent others. So, just as a position that suicide is always wrong is untenable, it is also implausible to insist that suicide can never be wrong.

A person with a terminal illness and a suicide bomber are clearly not representative of most suicides. Where a debilitating mental illness is present, which affects a person's reasoning, moral judgement of that suicide will also be inappropriate. Morality is traditionally concerned with the concept of agency and responsibility. In some mental illnesses, this is sufficiently compromised for the act in question not to be regarded as immoral or wrong.

That judgement can be passed in some cases should be stressed, however, as mental illness will not always be present. How then might suicides be assessed where mental illness is not a factor or only a minor issue? Certainly we can label some as wrong. In addition to the suicide bomber, consider the suicide of a healthy person who takes his life as a means of exacting revenge against an enemy, such as a former partner. Murder-suicides in the absence of mental illness often have an element of vengeance, such as in the case of a father who kills a child and then himself. This may be a double wrong.

Black-and-white assessments of self-killing as either right or wrong are often too restrictive, however. A complete consideration of all of the facts of a case and, in particular, any outstanding obligations and the consequences of the suicide on others should allow for other intermediate assessments to be reached. Suicide could be regarded as advisable, understandable, courageous, honourable, blameworthy or imprudent. It will certainly sometimes be appropriate to pass some form of negative judgment on someone who is not mentally incapacitated and takes their own life. They may show little regard for the distress that might be encountered by the person who finds their body or the subsequent agony experienced by their family and friends.

Suicide is, then, sometimes justified and sometimes wrong and intermediate assessments can also be reached.

Is There Such a Thing as Rational Suicide?

Suicide is one option available to someone who finds themself in a desperate predicament from which they wish to extricate themself. However, even in the case of a terminally ill person who is in constant pain, their right to kill themself does not mean that this is their best available option. For someone to conclude that it is their best option, they should assess the future course of their life, weigh up the likely positive and negative aspects and conclude that they would be better off dead. This cost-benefit-analysis-type approach to life makes many people uncomfortable.

Professor Ella Arensman has been involved in research into suicide and self-harm for over twenty-five years and says that, in all that time, she has never come across a rational suicide.[15] Having interviewed hundreds of people who have survived suicide attempts, she stresses that a choice of voluntary death is always ambiguous. Survivors mention reasons why they want to die while at the same time specifying why they want to live. Consultant psychiatrist Declan Murray accepts that a very small minority of suicides could be regarded as rational, but is troubled by the implications of this, since it likely requires society to regulate such suicides, which makes him uncomfortable. For others, the concept of rational suicide is nonsense, as they see suicide as the act of the depressed, hopeless person who is incapable of reasoning in a calm and objective manner.

How might the debate on rational suicide be resolved? Many suicides are clearly irrational. Someone who is experiencing a temporary bout of depression or who impulsively decides to kill themself because of some relatively minor mishap is clearly acting irrationally. The symptoms of mental illness mean that many unwell people are unable to objectively assess their current situation. When some other solution would have solved a person's problems – perhaps seeking treatment for an illness or addiction – death is obviously not the appropriate solution to their predicament.

Still, not all suicides are irrational. Support for this belief has come from surprising sources. In 1992, investigators from the Los Angeles Suicide-Prevention Centre analysed more than 700 suicide notes. The reasoning, judgement, and logic expressed in all of the notes was assessed, and the investigators concluded that 'a large minority of suicides, usually older persons in physical pain, are logical and rational and not psychotic'.[16]

Undoubtedly, a significant number of people rationally choose to end their own lives. The idea that people who endure a great deal of physical pain can reach such a decision is – though not accepted by everyone – a relatively uncontroversial idea. Establishing that someone with a mental illness can reach a similar rational decision to end their life is a different matter.

Dr Dermot Walsh, a consultant psychiatrist and former inspector of mental hospitals in Ireland, believes that some people who suffer from recurrent, seriously impairing mental illness can rationally decide to end their lives, although they only account for a small minority of suicides. Walsh points to people who have received treatment for their mental illness over a number of years, which has proven ineffective. An example of this would be a man who, during his adult life has had frequent long stays in mental-health inpatient facilities, closely monitored, perhaps restrained on a regular basis and left a shadow of his former self because of the medication that he must take to control his frequent psychotic delusions. Some aspects of his thinking may be irrational, but he can still rationally conclude that because of the debilitating effects of his illness, his quality of life will not improve and his life of misery is intolerable to him.

James L. Werth has suggested a set of criteria by which an assessment may be made as to whether a decision to complete suicide is rational.[17] A person must: have a hopeless condition, make the decision as a free choice of their own and have engaged in a sound decision-making process. There are five characteristics of a sound decision-making process. It should involve: consultation with a mental-health professional, a non-impulsive consideration of all alternatives, consideration of the congruence of the act with one's personal values, consideration of the impact on significant others and consultation with objective others and significant others.

Applying this set of criteria to the example provided by Walsh, let us consider whether a forty-year-old male who has lived with untreatable psychosis for more than twenty years might fulfil these criteria. Does he have a hopeless condition? Unlike a short-term episode of depression or other treatable mental illnesses, his condition can be regarded as hopeless on the basis that it cannot be treated and is associated with a very pessimistic prognosis. Werth's second criterion is a safeguard against incapacity and any pressure being exerted on a person. Someone with psychosis may not have the capacity to make such a decision to complete suicide but we must accept that he may – his diagnosis does not rule this out.

Werth's five characteristics of a rational decision-making process include additional safeguards. Consultation with a mental-health professional can ensure that treatable and reversible mental illness is not present. The impulsive nature of many suicides, which result from poorly thought-out decisions occurring in the midst of short-term crises, does not apply to our example.

Such a momentous decision should be in line with personal values. If a very ill man has strongly held religious beliefs that tell him that he should battle on and stay alive, he is unlikely to ever be comfortable with a decision to end his life and so should not proceed. The final two characteristics of the sound decision-making process ensure that he considers the impact of the suicide on others, such as family, friends and objective others, who may be other health professionals.

Implications for Suicide Prevention

Suicide-prevention strategies do not distinguish between suicides that are right and wrong or between rational and irrational suicides. It should seem obvious, though, that preventing an action that cannot be morally condemned or one which is the conclusion of a reasoned decision-making process is an arrogant imposition of a particular moral viewpoint. The irrational suicide should, on the other hand, always be prevented. If you come across someone in the act of attempting to kill themselves, a reasonable default strategy would be to try to stop that person from carrying out the act. More likely than not, you will be stopping someone from carrying out an irrational or impulsive act.

A mental-health social worker, Gavin Fairbairn, insists that a suicide-interventionist approach may be used in all instances in which we come across a potential suicide, on the basis of protecting ourselves and others.[18] He reflects, in particular, on the distressing effects of suicide on witnesses, as well as its effects on significant others. Fairbairn's reflections on the damage wreaked by suicide are similar, then, to McDaid's controversial sentiments.

Though unlikely, it is possible that a member of the public

may be able to recognise that a potential suicide has made a rational decision to kill themself. This member of the public may then decide not to intervene. The mental-health professional who encounters someone intent on killing themself does not have the same freedom to make one decision or the other. The professional must prevent all suicides, no matter how rational the decision-making process of the person is. There are ethical and legal responsibilities that override their personal beliefs and values, and require them to do their upmost to prevent all deaths. Any decision by a professional not to intervene in a suicide attempt could carry legal consequences and lead to professional ruin. Professionals should have a wider array of options available to them, but until the legitimacy of rational suicide is given legal recognition, their choices are limited.

Like individuals and mental-health professionals, the state should prevent irrational and impulsive suicides, although it has a set of additional considerations. Suicides harm society by leading to more suicides. Productive members of society are lost. It is in the state's interest to assume a preventative and aftercare role towards suicidal persons who are not acting rationally. However, its laws should not allow the involuntary detention of such people based on overstated, unrealistic assessments of the likelihood that they will harm themselves.

Where societies conduct debates on issues surrounding suicide and reach conclusions, the state must legislate based on these outcomes. The experiences of Oregon and the Netherlands suggest that any relaxation of the laws on suicide will be a gradual process. Parliaments will likely first legislate for assisted suicide with appropriate safeguards when the moral case for such a right becomes more widely accepted. Ultimately, the role of legislation should be to allow for effective preventative measures to be put in place to thwart the actions of the irrational or impulsive person. Where we can successfully prevent such a person from ending their life, they should be provided with an opportunity to undertake a more measured and reasoned analysis of their predicament in time. Hopefully, we can provide them with whatever help might assist them to overcome their difficulties.

We must allow, though, that suicides will still occur. On rare occasions, a retrospective judgement that an individual suicide was a wrongful act will be justified – but this may be hurtful to families and unnecessarily cruel. On the other hand, retrospectively glorifying or condoning the act might encourage others. The best course is to adopt a compassionate, understanding and understated position, especially considering the frailty of some individuals.

10.
An Introduction
to Suicide Prevention

Societies and religions have historically prohibited suicide using arguments that focus on the intrinsic wrongness of killing. Another powerful historical argument against suicide was that the individual belongs to the state or to God and has no right to interfere with the property of either. This type of prohibition certainly had some preventative effect. The brutal treatment of the bodies of suicide victims and families that was associated with laws against suicide meant, however, that it came to be regarded as unnecessarily cruel. Most churches do not regard suicide as sinful nowadays, and most societies do not regard it as a crime. Modern approaches to suicide prevention that involve openly discussing and disseminating information about what were once taboo topics also enjoy significant public support.

Though a strong case can be made that a tiny proportion of all suicides – rational suicides – should not be prevented, concerted efforts to prevent the overwhelming majority of self-inflicted deaths have significant moral weight behind them. The stories of men like John Quinn and Eddie D'Alton reveal to us the shattering impact that suicide has on families. Most suicides clearly do not result from reasoned consideration of alternatives.

Society should, then, support efforts that can keep people alive to enjoy better times ahead and that can also prevent friends and family members from having to endure pain, suffering and guilt.

There are many other reasons why effective suicide-prevention activities should be championed. Intervene and prevent someone in the midst of an acute suicidal crisis from taking their life and we know that they are very unlikely to go on to kill themself later. In 1974, Richard Seiden examined what happened to 515 people who were prevented from jumping from the Golden Gate Bridge in San Francisco over the course of thirty-five years. Only twenty-five of them (less than 5 percent) subsequently ended their own lives.[1]

Sometimes people instantly regret their suicidal decisions. The story of suicide-prevention campaigner Kevin Hines was featured in Eric Steel's documentary film, *The Bridge*. The film describes the lives of a number of people who died after leaping from San Francisco's iconic bridge and controversially includes actual footage of a number of jumps. Hines actually survived his jump in September 2000, one of only a handful of people to have cheated death in this way. He now emphasises that he regretted his decision as soon as he jumped and prayed to God that he would survive. Somehow, he did. Suicide is also contagious. Prevent someone from killing themself and there is a strong likelihood that we will avert the future suicide of a friend or family member of theirs.

Professor Ella Arensman stressed to us the ambiguity that suicidal people feel about dying. This is why many seek help. They want to stay alive but want to get rid of all the pain and suffering in their lives. When suicide-prevention efforts are supported, governments, communities and individuals are saying that they are prepared to help distressed people stay alive.

The belief that almost all suicides are linked to mental illness has meant, however, that a huge degree of responsibility for the prevention of suicides has fallen on mental-health professionals. Mental illness is, of course, associated with many suicides. And yet, the likelihood is that even when mental illness largely explains a death, other factors are also involved. The need to address all the factors that influence suicide makes prevention very difficult.

Even if mental-health professionals knew how to prevent suicides amongst this high-risk group (the mentally ill), they are unsure who they should target with such preventative measures. They are unable to accurately predict who is at highest risk and who will go on to kill themself. A reliance on the mental-health-care system will clearly be insufficient if the problem of suicide is to be comprehensively tackled. It will also fail to prevent most suicides, even among those who are mentally ill.

British initiatives in the late nineteenth and early twentieth century recognised the folly of relying on the treatment of mental illness to stop suicides; the London Anti-Suicide Bureau urged anyone who had suicidal thoughts to make contact. But it was not until Finland implemented the world's first national suicide-prevention strategy in the early 1990s that a broad-based prevention programme was developed for national implementation.

The Finnish strategy was a response to the country's persistent high suicide rate. It assumed that a concerted effort to prevent suicides required activity in multiple domains. Care and treatment for people with mental illness were important components. The strategy also funded campaigns to reduce the stigma surrounding the use of mental-health and suicide-prevention services. What was especially notable about the initiative was that it also included actions in areas as diverse as the labour market, the education system and the media.

As well as including specific measures to target those at increased risk of suicide, the Finnish strategy adopted a public-health approach, attempting to reduce risk factors for suicide in the general population. Following the Finnish example, there is now an established international consensus that implementing broad-based prevention strategies is how the complex problem of suicide can best be addressed. The United States Surgeon General and the National Action Alliance for Suicide Prevention jointly developed a new national strategy for suicide prevention for the United States in 2012, for example. England also launched a new suicide-prevention strategy in 2012.

In light of this international consensus, one might assume that the actions recommended by suicide-prevention strategies would actually deliver concrete results. An honest assessment must, however, recognise that the evidence to support most of the initiatives routinely used to prevent suicide is lacking. A 2012 evaluation carried out for the World Health Organization of sui-cide-prevention strategies and interventions found that the evidence for the effectiveness of national suicide programmes was 'scant and equivocal'.[2] Studies have suggested that implementation of the original Finnish strategy led to a sharp fall in the country's suicide rate, but there is no evidence from other countries that national suicide-prevention strategies have had any impact on the number of people talking their own lives.

This pessimistic finding needs to be considered in the context of how difficult it is to show that a particular intervention or programme prevents suicide. Showing that an intervention saved one or two lives will not do. We need evidence from robust research that can point to decreases in the rate of suicide within the general population. Proving through a randomised controlled trial that a specific intervention reduces the overall suicide rate is especially challenging. Because the base rate of suicide is so low, thousands of participants need to be recruited into such trials in order to determine the effectiveness of interventions. For ethical reasons, many people who are assessed at being at high risk of suicide are not regularly recruited into such trials.

These challenges mean that suicide researchers have had to make do with alternative approaches. Rather than looking at entire populations, they commonly concentrate on specific groups. There are many studies that focus, for instance, on high-risk groups such as those who have made a suicide attempt and people with certain mental illnesses. Results show that certain interventions can be effective in preventing suicides within such groups. But we must stress that this does not show that they will make any difference to population suicide rates.

Another approach sees suicide researchers looking beyond changes in the numbers of actual suicides. It is much easier to check whether interventions alter the prevalence of more-common suicidal behaviours, such as suicide attempts and deliberate self-harm. Obviously, any intervention that has been shown to reduce suicidal behaviour in the general population or in high-risk groups must be supported. But we must not shy away from acknowledging the limitations of these approaches. Most of the time, we have to acknowledge that they may have no impact on the numbers of actual suicides in the country as a whole. The limitations of our knowledge about the impacts of interventions that can reduce known risk factors for suicide (such as depression and stress) and enhance protective factors (such as self-esteem) are greater still. Such programmes clearly demonstrate benefits, but to deduce that they prevent suicides is bad science.

No strong evidence exists, then, to support most of the actions common to suicide-prevention strategies. This realistic assessment of the state of our current knowledge regarding suicide-prevention shapes our analysis, but we intend to offer a more optimistic message by primarily concentrating in the next two chapters on interventions that have some evidence to support their effectiveness. In most cases, this evidence does not reach the gold standard that we would aspire to, but we will not ignore interventions if a considered analysis of research findings indicates that they can be effective in reducing population suicide rates.

The effectiveness of restricting access to the methods commonly used in suicides has been reported as a 'best practice' in different systematic reviews,[3,4] and we will focus on this promising area in detail in the next chapter. We will also touch on interventions that have been proven to reduce suicide or suicidal behaviours among specific groups. We will point out that because an evidence vacuum exists with respect to how to deal with many people in a suicidal crisis, approaches based on reason, logic and common sense cannot be ignored.

11.
Suicide Prevention: What Works?
Universal Preventative Measures

We all rely on population health strategies to keep us healthy and free from disease. A variety of laws and regulations ensure that we have access to safe drinking water and that employers must take steps to protect our health and safety at work. A public-health model that targets the health and well-being of each and every one of us can also extend to reducing the number of people who die in the lonely circumstances of suicide.

Most people who end their lives will never have made a suicide attempt or come to the attention of mental-health professionals or crisis services. The impulsive nature of many suicide fatalities means that people who are categorised as low-risk still go on to end their lives. They represent a small proportion of the low-risk population but still make a significant contribution to the total number of deaths from suicide. If overall suicide rates and numbers are going to be reduced, suicide-prevention initiatives that target everyone are clearly required.

Restricting physical access to the methods commonly used by people to end their lives and reducing overall alcohol consumption are two of the most effective ways that we can cut deaths from suicide.

Means Restriction

Surprise and doubt are two common reactions encountered when you tell people that restricting access to lethal methods can be a successful way of curbing deaths. They reason that laws might be introduced that make it more difficult to access a certain method but frequently assume that the determined person will simply find another way to take their life.

When Olive Anderson evaluated means-restriction efforts in Victorian and Edwardian England, she concluded that these efforts were an almost unwinnable battle against technological progress. Though she acknowledged that suicide by some of the methods that were restricted decreased, she believed that the emergence of newer ways for people to kill themselves cancelled out whatever progress might have been made. She pointed to the birth of the railway as an example. Most recent evidence suggests, however, that when access to suicide methods is limited, only a minority of people switch to alternatives.

Voltaire speculated that, 'the man who, in a fit of melancholy, kills himself today, would have wished to live had he waited a week'.[1] The strategy of means restriction accepts that this is usually the case. It is aimed at people who have moved beyond thinking about killing themselves towards planning a suicide attempt. Physically preventing them from carrying out the fatal act must take precedence until the suicide crisis passes.

The evidence available from a variety of population studies indicates that means restriction is an effective way of reducing the overall suicide rate. It has also been shown to reduce suicide rates among specific groups and to cut suicide attempts and other forms of suicidal behaviours. Let's begin by looking at the example offered by England and Wales's experience with coal gas half a century ago.

Coal-Gas

At the end of the 1950s, roughly half of all suicides in England and Wales involved domestic gas – some 2,500 suicides per year. Victims simply opened their ovens and inhaled the gas. Because it was derived from coal, the gas had very high levels of carbon monoxide, so this often proved fatal.

In her well-known novel, *The Bell Jar*, Sylvia Plath wrote that 'the trouble about jumping was that if you didn't pick the right number of stories, you might still be alive when you hit bottom.'[2] Such thoughts may have been what prompted her to choose to stick her head in the oven when deciding to end her life in 1963.

New technology allowed gas to be produced with much lower levels of carbon monoxide from 1958 onwards. By the time England and Wales had switched to cleaner North Sea natural gas by 1977, carbon monoxide levels in gas were close to zero. When the detoxification programme began, little reference was made to its likely impact on suicide numbers. The impact was substantial, though.

Suicides by domestic gas declined in England and Wales, from 2,368 in 1963 to twenty-three in 1975. There was a 5 per-cent increase in suicides using other methods during the same period, much lower than might have been expected.[3] This meant that the overall suicide rate decreased by 40 percent in these years and that there were 2,021 fewer suicides. The suicide rate fell for both men and women and for all age groups. As with all ecological data, we cannot be certain that gas detoxification caused the substantial decline in suicides, but the very different pattern observed for suicides involving other methods strongly suggests that it was the crucial factor.

Figure 11.1 | Suicides in England and Wales, 1960-1975

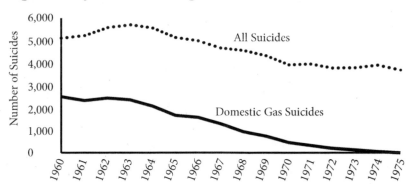

Source: Clarke, R. V. and Mayhew, P. 'Crime as Opportunity: A Note on Domestic Gas Suicide in Britain and the Netherlands'. In the *British Journal of Criminology, Delinquency and Deviant Social Behaviour.* 1989; (29) 1.

Pesticides

Success in cutting suicide numbers through means restriction should be much more likely if we can limit access to a method that is popular, easily available and lethal. Pesticides fulfil all three criteria in many poorer countries. In rural regions of Asia, Africa and Latin America, especially, weed killers, insecticides and herbicides are commonly used in farming and are relatively easy to access. Though rarely used in suicidal acts in the West, they account for 30 percent of global suicides each year, so they are the most common method worldwide. They are highly toxic. Some pesticides kill as many as 60 percent of those who ingest them. Restricting access to these deadly chemicals has a very important role to play in global suicide-prevention efforts.

Sri Lanka has illustrated just how effective limiting access to deadly pesticides can be. Beginning in 1984, its government banned two insecticides and then phased out all other extremely or highly toxic pesticides between 1991 and 1995. An import ban on these came into effect in July 1995. It was followed by a further import ban in 1998 on moderately toxic pesticides. A study by David Gunnell and his co-authors showed that these measures were associated with a fall of 50 percent in the country's suicide rate between 1996 and 2005. Almost 20,000 fewer Sri Lankans ended their lives by suicide during these years than had done so in the previous ten years.[4] Because theirs was an ecological study, Gunnell and his co-authors examined alternative explanations for the dramatic decline in suicide. These included unemployment, levels of alcohol use, the prevalence of divorce and the country's long-running civil war, which only came to an end in 2009. None of these factors appeared to be associated with the fall in suicides.[5]

Guns

Guns are used in half of all suicides in the United States. Unsurprisingly, they are also highly lethal. More than four out of five (84 percent) of those who shoot themselves will not survive.[6] Though liberal firearms legislation in the United States means that guns are generally easily available, gun-ownership levels in the United States are far from uniform. In 2002, for example, 5 percent of households in Washington DC had a firearm, but a staggering 63 percent in Wyoming did.[7]

Matthew Miller and a number of research colleagues suspected that suicide rates would be much higher in US states with high levels of gun ownership than in states where fewer people owned guns. So they compared suicides in the fifteen US states with the highest levels of household gun ownership with suicides in the six US states with the lowest levels of household gun ownership. The make-up of the two groups of states was such that their total population sizes were similar: 39 million in the first group and 40 million in the second. Average household gun ownership was just 15 percent in the low-gun-ownership group, compared to 47 percent in the high-gun-ownership group. The researchers then examined suicide numbers over the three-year period from 2000 to 2002.[8]

From 2000 to 2002, the total numbers of suicides involving methods other than guns was similar in the two groups: 5,060 in the high-gun-ownership states and 5,446 in the low gun-owner-ship states. However, there were three times as many suicides involving guns in the states with high gun ownership as in the states with low gun ownership (see Figure 11.2). The impact of this was that the total number of suicides in the high-gun-own-ership states (14,809) was almost twice the total number of sui-cides (8,052) in the low-gun-ownership states.

Figure 11.2 | Suicides in High Gun-Ownership States vs. Low Gun-Ownership States, 2000-2002

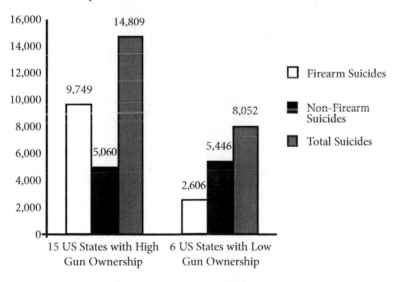

Source: Miller, M., Lippmann, S. J., Azrael, D. and Hemenway, D. 'Household Firearm Ownership and Rates of Suicide Across the Fifty United States'. In *Journal of Trauma-Injury Infection and Critical Care*. 2007; (62) 4: pp1029-1035.

As the number of suicides using methods other than guns was more or less the same in each of the two groups of states, it is reasonable to assume that the suicidal intent of the two populations was also more or less the same and that, as a result, so was the number of suicide attempts. The difference between the suicide rates of the two groups of states is, of course, much more likely to be because large numbers of people living in the first group of states have easy access to a highly lethal means of killing themselves. This results in a higher rate of suicide involving guns, which likely explains the substantial difference between the numbers of people taking their lives in the different groups of states. Where there is more gun ownership, there is more suicide.

Gun-control debates in the United States typically gather momentum following a firearms-related mass murder. Remarkably, though, these gun-control debates rarely focus on suicide, in spite of the fact that roughly twice as many Americans die of self-inflicted gunshot wounds every year than are murdered with firearms. It is like pondering the risks tobacco poses to population health by focusing on cardiovascular health, while ignoring cancer.

If we could restrict access to guns through legislation, though, would it reduce suicide? Experience suggests that the answer is yes – both suicides involving guns and overall suicide rates should decline. One of the reasons for the relatively low levels of gun ownership in Washington DC is that it introduced some of the most restrictive gun laws in the United States in 1976 (some elements of which were struck down by a 2008 Supreme Court ruling). The Firearms Control Regulations Act forbade residents from owning a range of weapons, including handguns and automatic firearms. Those who kept guns in their homes had to keep them unloaded and make sure they were fitted with trigger locks.

When researchers tracked the average monthly rate of suicide in Washington DC before and after the introduction of the law, from 1968 through to 1987, they found that it decreased by 23 percent following the introduction of the law.[9] There was no increase in suicides involving other methods. Again, it is possible that other reasons may have accounted for the recorded decrease, but such findings have been replicated in studies that looked at the impact of gun-control measures outside of the United States.

Switzerland offers another example. Beginning in March 2003, Switzerland cut its army in half over the course of a year. One knock-on effect of this was a dramatic reduction in the number of guns stored in Swiss homes. Thomas Reisch and three research colleagues speculated that this might have lead to a decrease in suicides, especially among young men. So they examined population (ecological) data.

Reisch and his colleagues showed that the reduction in the number of guns stored in Swiss homes was associated with a reduction in the suicide rate involving guns and in the overall suicide rate among men between the ages of eighteen and forty-three.[10] There were 2.2 fewer suicides per 100,000 people for men in this age group in the years 2004 to 2008 than there would have been if the trends of the years 1995 to 2003 had continued. The authors strengthened their study by matching men in this age group with two control groups: men aged forty-four and fifty-three and women aged eighteen to forty-four. No changes in suicide rates in these two groups were found.

Why Is Means Restriction Often So Successful?

Targeting popular, highly lethal and easily available means of suicide is a successful strategy, but why does it work? Many decisions to die by one's own hand are taken impulsively. How hastily such decisions can be taken was revealed by Thomas Simon and his colleagues when they interviewed 153 survivors of nearly lethal suicide attempts in Houston, Texas.[11] Survivors of nearly lethal attempts are people who tried to kill themselves using methods that usually kill, such as hanging and firearms. They are an especially useful group to study, as they should be very similar to those who die by suicide.

Simon and others asked all of the survivors, aged between thirteen and thirty-four, to indicate how much time had elapsed between the moment they decided to kill themselves and the moment they actually carried out the attempt. For a quarter of those interviewed, less than five minutes elapsed between the decision and the attempt. For 71 percent, less than an hour had elapsed. Only 13 percent of those interviewed had attempted suicide a day or more after making that decision. German footballer Robert Enke is likely to have been someone who fell into this latter group.

When a person has easy access to a lethal means of suicide in a situation where they are acting impulsively and not thinking rationally, the consequences will often be fatal. Making it more difficult for such a person to access a highly lethal method often provides time for the suicidal crisis to pass, saving their life. Some suicidal crises are very brief.

Since many people have a preference for a specific means of suicide, when a barrier is put in their way in the short term, they are unlikely to switch to another method. A powerful Swedish study followed more than 48,000 people admitted to hospital following an attempted suicide between 1973 and 1982. It found that most of those who went on to kill themselves did so using the same method they had tried during their first attempt.[12] Where the first suicide attempt was made by hanging, for example, 93 percent of men and 92 percent of women who went on to kill themselves died by hanging.

Some would-be suicide completers are obsessed with a specific method, to the point that they cannot consider another way to die. One survivor of an attempt to leap from the Golden Gate Bridge recounted to Richard Seiden his determination to take his life by jumping from the western side of the iconic bridge.[13] He aroused the attention of passers-by because of his erratic behaviour on the eastern side of the bridge, and they stopped him. The man's problem was that he had decided to jump from a spot on the western side of the bridge and between him and his chosen location were six lanes of traffic. He just could not see how he could make his way there. He was afraid he would be knocked down by a car.

Not everyone has a preference for a specific suicide method. But means restriction can still work. If, for example, a person finds themself unable to jump from their preferred bridge, because it now has a safety barrier installed, will they take their life in some other way? Will they be able to organise this? They may not be able to think clearly enough during their suicidal crisis to complete the suicide using another method. If they do make an attempt but are forced to use a less-deadly method, they are more likely to survive.

Alcohol

Dr Dermot Walsh says alcohol nowadays acts as a 'potent fuel', spurring people – and young men, in particular – to act on suicidal impulses.[14] He believes that consuming alcohol when facing a sudden, relatively minor trauma or frustration can lead them to react impulsively and kill themselves without thinking things through properly. The short-term role that alcohol plays in self-inflicted death is shown in studies where the blood-alcohol levels of people who have taken their lives are examined. For example, tests carried out on more than 2,000 people over the age of fifteen who died by suicide in the US state of Oklahoma between 1997 and 2001 revealed that around one-third (32 percent) had elevated blood-alcohol levels.[15] A Swedish study from 2010 reported that a similar percentage (34 percent) of suicides had recently consumed alcohol.[16]

As with the abuse of other substances, there are fluctuations of mood associated with intoxication and withdrawal from alcohol. In these circumstances, many people hit rock-bottom, and suicide can seem an appealing option. Someone who abuses alcohol over the long term increases their risk of suicide. We also know that a society's overall level of alcohol consumption influences its suicide rate. In a 2011 study, Dermot Walsh and Brendan Walsh sought to explain the suicide rate in Ireland over a forty-year period by linking it to the country's unemployment rate and its level of alcohol consumption.[17] They found that high rates of unemployment and high levels of alcohol consumption between 1968 and 2009 were associated with an increased suicide rate, but that the effect of alcohol consumption on the suicide rate was especially pronounced for men up to the age of sixty-four. Drinking alcohol, then, increases risk for individuals both in the short term and in the long term, and a society's level of alcohol consumption is linked to suicide.

Although he is feted in the West for his policies of *perestroika* (restructuring) and *glasnost* (openness), Mikhail Gorbachev's introduction in 1985 of a tough anti-alcohol campaign that was associated with a substantial reduction in suicides in the USSR is less well-known. The consumption of alcohol – and of vodka, in particular – had strong cultural and historic roots, especially in the Slavic and Baltic regions of the Soviet Union. Men were especially heavy drinkers. Communist Party policy aimed to drastically reduce consumption through a series of measures.[18] Only coupons could be used to buy alcohol and purchases were limited to half a litre of 40 percent alcohol volume per person per month. Price was also used to influence demand; the coupon price of vodka increased from nine roubles per litre to nineteen roubles per litre.

Sales data collected from state sources shows that consumption decreased by 57 percent across the fifteen Soviet republics between 1984 and 1988.[19] Unsurprisingly, many Soviets went to great efforts to get alcohol from unofficial sources, much as Americans did during their period of Prohibition. Home brews were common. There are estimates that take account of unofficial sales, though, and such estimates for the Russian republic of the Soviet Union also show a steep fall in the amount of alcohol consumed. Overall consumption still fell by 25 percent between 1984 and 1986, from 14.2 litres to 10.6 litres per person per year, before it began to increase gradually. Certainly, after 1988, the policy lost much of its impetus, not least because a series of budget deficits affected the state's enthusiasm for it. Following the break-up of the USSR, consumption soared again.

Figure 11.3 | Consumption of Alcohol in Russia in Litres Per Capita, 1984-1989

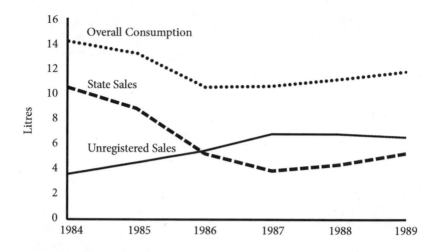

Source: Ryan, M. 'Russian Report: Alcoholism and Rising Mortality in the Russian Federation'. In *BMJ*. 1995; 310 (648).

Suicide rates in the twenty-year period prior to Gorbachev's assumption of power had been relatively stable throughout the Soviet Union, with Russia and the other Slavic republics accounting for the bulk of the suicide numbers. A substantial decline in suicide throughout the USSR coincided with the period of *perestroika* and the fall in alcohol consumption, according to research by Dr Airi Varnik, an Estonian psychiatrist and suicide researcher.

With colleagues, Varnik, who played an active part in the anti-alcohol campaign as a doctor in what was then Soviet Estonia, has since then studied the association between suicide rates and declines in alcohol consumption.[20] Varnik has shown that suicide rates decreased across the USSR during *perestroika* –

the rate for men fell by a third (32 percent). The largest decreases occurred in Russia and Belarus, where the male suicide rate fell by 42 percent. Suicide rates also fell in other European countries at this time, but not as dramatically. It is revealing that the decline was particularly pronounced for men, who accounted for the vast majority of alcohol consumption.

As with other studies of this kind, we cannot establish for certain that the reduction in the amount of alcohol consumed caused the decline in suicide. Other social and political reforms that were sweeping across the USSR during the final years before its break up may also have been relevant. Gorbachev's anti-alcohol crusade is, however, the most likely explanation and this reasoning is buttressed by the fact that a significant decline in the overall suicide rate in Iceland also followed reforms that were made to the regulation of alcohol in that country.[21]

★

Curtailing access to the physical means of suicide and to alcohol and other substances are not the only universal initiatives included in national suicide-prevention strategies. Promoting the responsible reporting of suicidal behaviour in the media is another, although, as we have seen, it may be necessary to curtail reporting altogether in order to curtail the suicide contagion associated with media coverage of the phenomenon.

The evidence base for most universal measures that are routinely implemented is lacking. We just cannot say for certain that even what appear to be 'common-sense' interventions work. These include educating the general public about depression and training 'gatekeepers'. The latter strategy equips people such as schoolteachers, police officers and clergy – who may come into contact with vulnerable people – with the 'skills' to detect those who may be at risk so that they can refer them onto sources of help.

Two universal preventive evidence-based measures can be recommended, though: means restriction and reducing a society's level of alcohol consumption. Both were initially suggested as ways of curtailing suicide in the late nineteenth century. How disappointing it is that more than a century of research and investigation since then has not significantly advanced our knowledge of other effective measures that target everyone. Suicide's complexity and the inherent challenges associated with preventing it explain the static nature of our knowledge.

12.
Suicide Prevention: What Works?
Interventions for Those
at Increased Risk

You are a busy psychiatrist in the middle of a weekend shift and you have just assessed a patient who has engaged in impulsive suicidal behaviour for the first time. He took an overdose of his mother's tablets while drunk, after a row with his girlfriend. After the assessment, you are clear, however, that he does not have a mental illness and so will not benefit from the admission to hospital that his family are pressurising you to organise. You believe that there is a slim chance that he will make another attempt soon, but you are aware of the flaws associated with predicting risk. An image flashes through your mind of a patient that you classified as low-risk, who later died from suicide. You become fearful of the repercussions if this patient kills himself following the discharge that you initially thought best for him. What do you do?

The traditional response of many doctors in this situation has been to hospitalise the patient. An inpatient facility often will be the most appropriate place for someone in the midst of a suicidal crisis to access care and treatment. Usually, however, this will only apply when the suicidal crisis is associated with a serious mental illness that will benefit from treatment in such a facility. It must be stressed that hospitalisation is frequently inappropriate. However, the patient's family is relieved, the doctor has less reason to worry about a potential suicide occurring in the short term and the belief that admitting suicidal people to hospital saves lives is reinforced.

Has admitting the patient really helped to save a life? It is possible that an admission can reduce the likelihood of a suicide occurring in an individual case in the short term. At the same time, suicides still occur in restrictive inpatient facilities. Very significantly, there is no proof that hospitalisation actually reduces suicide. The difficulty, as perceived by consultant psychiatrist Declan Murray, is that people in a suicidal crisis need to learn to solve the problem that is driving this suicidal crisis. Admission to hospital, however, immediately switches off all problem-solving behaviour. People in crisis are, if you like, passive recipients of care. This pattern tends to get repeated when they encounter difficulties again.[1]

Where, then, should someone experiencing a suicidal crisis go? What intervention should the clinician or concerned family member recommend so that the person might be kept alive? This will depend on many factors: the presence or absence of mental illness; whether the suicidal crisis has been accompanied by a suicidal act; what services are available around the person; and, crucially, whether there is evidence that the service or intervention can reduce suicide or suicidal behaviour.

The remainder of this chapter concentrates primarily on the limited number of interventions that have been shown to be effective in reducing suicidal behaviour and suicide among some groups of people who are at increased risk. There is no suggestion that answers are provided to all of the potential difficult situations that clinicians and family members of people in crisis may encounter. The limited number of interventions we recommend includes dialectical behaviour therapy (DBT), a form of psychotherapy for people with borderline personality disorder (BPD), a diagnosis that is associated with chronic self-harming behaviour. The medication lithium reduces suicide among people with depression and other mood disorders.

What of the person in immediate crisis, however, who needs help now? Follow-up contacts and a safety-planning intervention can be appropriate for people who have sought assistance. They have been used with suicide attempters who have sought help and can also be used by the clinician faced with someone in crisis in an emergency department. We classify the safety-planning intervention as an optimistic intervention because, although, it is currently the subject of ongoing randomised controlled trials, there is as yet no solid evidence showing that it reduces suicide or suicidal behaviour. Elements of it are based on solid evidence from elsewhere, however, and it provides an opportunity for friends and relatives of a suicidal person to play a role (along with a professional) in keeping a vulnerable person safe.

Dialectical Behaviour Therapy (DBT)

DBT was developed by Marsha Linehan in the United States primarily for chronically suicidal female patients with BPD. Around 9 percent of those with BPD eventually kill themselves and 70 percent will attempt suicide at least once. Threats of suicide are frequently made by the typical borderline patient and so, unsurprisingly, those treating her frequently find the experience extremely stressful. Women account for between 75 and 90 percent of patients with BPD. It was the diagnosis that best described the condition experienced by the young Linehan, which led to her being hospitalised for the first time at the age of seventeen.

Such was the extent of Linehan's own self-harming behaviour during her first stay in hospital that she became the sole occupant of the seclusion room on her unit. She regularly burnt herself with cigarettes, slashed her arms and cut herself all over at every opportunity. Unable to cut herself in the barren seclusion room, she repeatedly banged her head against the wall and floor.[2] When she was eventually discharged, her hospital records stated that, 'during twenty-six months of hospitalisation, Miss Linehan was, for a considerable part of this time, one of the most disturbed patients in the hospital.'[3] Linehan eventually recovered, earned a PhD in psychology and went on to develop a revolutionary therapy.

A number of randomised controlled trials (RCTs) have shown evidence for the effectiveness of Linehan's methods of reducing suicide attempts and self-harming behaviour, although these trials have had small numbers of participants. In the first-ever RCT on Linehan's method, involving forty-four women who exhibited frequent self harming behaviour, the findings showed that compared to treatment as usual, women who received DBT had lower rates of suicide attempts and other self-harming behaviour as well as lower rates of hospitalisation. They also stayed in treatment for longer.[4]

A subsequent trial was especially noteworthy because the members of the control group, who did not receive DBT, were treated by therapists regarded as experts in treating patients with borderline personality disorder.[5] This study of 101 women found that the DBT group of patients had lower rates of suicide attempts and hospitalisation. They also showed a lower medical risk of self-harming behaviour, displayed less angry behaviour and had fewer emergency-room visits than the control group.

Borderline patients experience extreme mood swings, depression and anger. They have difficulty controlling their emotions, act impulsively and experience difficulties in relationships. With this astonishing multitude of problems, it is no wonder that these patients were traditionally regarded as untreatable. Of all of the characteristics of BPD, it is the inability to control emotions that Linehan identifies as the primary problem. This may have a genetic component and be linked to the environment in which the borderline patient was raised.

One of Linehan's insights was to view the problematic behaviours associated with the diagnosis as resulting from an interaction between a poorly regulated emotional system and what she terms an invalidating environment. Displays of anger, distress or other negative emotions may have seen someone with BPD ignored or punished. Confusion abounds for the patient, though, when cutting herself and other extreme behaviours attract comforting attention. Over time, her ability to communicate and regulate her emotions can become so impaired that she relies on self-harming behaviour to regulate emotions. The core problem-solving behaviour that DBT, therefore, tries to instil in patients is learning how to control their emotions.

DBT grew out of standard cognitive behavioural therapy (CBT), another form of psychotherapy that is still used to treat mental illness and people who are suicidal. The primary goal of CBT is to get patients to alter unhealthy patterns of thinking and behaviour. Linehan originally worked with CBT, but found that its emphasis on change strategies was not best-suited to patients with BPD. They often withdrew from treatment or attacked the therapist, seeing the emphasis on change as meaning that their problems were not properly understood. A further difficulty was the sheer scale and nature of problems that the patients presented with. This made it almost impossible for an individual therapist to address these multiple problems and also have sufficient time to teach the patient newer skills that they so desperately needed.[6]

From these observations, DBT was born, placing a particular emphasis on the need to balance change and acceptance strategies. Radical acceptance means understanding that the patient's extreme behaviour, including self-harm, makes sense. Long disillusioned by traditional therapists, Linehan realised that acceptance strategies were essential so that patients finally felt that their experiences were validated. They were then much more likely to engage in treatment. Change strategies in DBT share the same aims of CBT in terms of teaching patients alternative ways of dealing with their problems, including having them realise that although self-harming behaviour makes sense at the time, it is not in their long-term interests. This tension between change and acceptance is the essential dialectic or contradiction in DBT. Building a successful alliance between therapist and patient can eventually gain a commitment from the patient to change her behaviour.

DBT treatment is structured by a series of priorities and targets that are dealt with in order of importance. Typically, at the start of a programme of DBT, the priorities are to reduce life-threatening and self-harming behaviours before moving on to behaviours that interfere with therapy, and then behaviours that affect the patient's quality of life.

A unique feature of DBT is the use of therapists' consultation groups, in which DBT therapists discuss the issues that emerge during therapy on a weekly basis. Partly designed to deal with the stressful nature of work with chronically suicidal patients, it is also a forum for therapists to seek advice from one other on how best to progress with treatment. Telephone crisis coaching facilitates the patient contacting the therapist outside of therapy as a means for her to seek assistance if she is in crisis or wants some advice on how to use some particular aspect of DBT.

The evidence for DBT's effectiveness that has come from randomised controlled trials prompted the UK's National Institute of Health and Clinical Excellence (NICE) to recommend DBT as the treatment of choice for women with BPD who want to reduce their self-harming behaviour. Though designed primarily for those who are chronically suicidal, it has been successfully adapted for use with other groups, such as adolescents, people with eating disorders and a variety of depressed patients. Further trials have shown DBT to be effective in treating substance abuse among patients with dual diagnoses of BPD and substance-use disorders.

The usual treatment model involves delivering DBT in an outpatient setting – typically for a year and sometimes longer – but it can also form part of an inpatient-treatment programme. It is not at all clear how DBT works, although it seems likely that the skills that it transfers to borderline patients equip them with a set of strategies which, when implemented, enable them to reduce the impact of stressful events that would have previously led them to engage in self-harming behaviour.

Lithium

In the early twentieth century, before its mood-stabilising properties were discovered, the naturally occurring element lithium was used to treat a variety of physical conditions, including heart disease. It was also used in an early version of the soft drink 7 Up. Extreme side effects and a number of deaths associated with its use, however, culminated in a sales ban in 1949.

Reports of lithium's effectiveness in treating people with mental illness were, therefore, initially treated with caution. Since the late 1960s, though, it has been successfully used to treat a range of mood disorders, especially bipolar disorder. We know that it is poisonous in large quantities, so it must be used with great caution. Dosage must also be regularly monitored through blood tests because of its potential to cause long-term damage to the kidneys and thyroid gland.

Notwithstanding all of these potential nasty side effects, lithium is the one medication that has a very strong anti-suicide effect. A systematic review of a number of randomised controlled trials compared lithium with other treatments, including medically ineffective placebo treatments. It examined whether treatment with lithium for at least twelve months reduced deaths by suicide or other causes. It also looked at the impact on rates of self-harm.[7]

Outcomes for more than 6,600 patients were included and the study found unequivocally that compared to a placebo, treatment with lithium reduces death from suicide by an average of 87 percent. The evidence that treatment with lithium reduces deliberate self-harm was less clear-cut. We know that personality traits such and aggression and impulsivity are associated with suicide.

Lithium can decrease both, which may explain why it reduces the risk of suicide.

Follow-Up Contacts

When it is time for those who have sought and received treatment following a suicide attempt to go home, a scenario similar to what was presented at the beginning of the chapter confronts the clinician. The patient needs to be discharged, but it is well-established that someone who has made a suicide attempt is at increased risk, especially during the first weeks after discharge. Most inpatient units, then, try to arrange follow-up appointments with patients as soon as possible after their discharge.

Now it seems that we have evidence that the relatively straightforward intervention of proactively making follow-up contacts post discharge can reduce suicides and suicidal behaviour. A comprehensive 2013 review by David Luxton, Jennifer June and Katherine Comtois focused on interventions such as follow-up contacts.[8] All but one of the eleven studies they investigated were randomised trials that concentrated on inpatient psychiatric patients or emergency-room patients who were being discharged to their homes. The review of all of the studies did not conclusively show that these contacts work definitively, but it found that on balance, they should be promoted.

One of the trials Luxton and his research team reviewed was organised by the WHO in eight hospitals in five different countries.[9] Centres in Brazil, India, Sri Lanka, Iran and China participated in the study, which lasted from January 2002 to October 2005 and sought to establish whether the provision of a brief information session close to discharge from an emergency department, accompanied by nine follow-up contacts, consisting of telephone calls or involving face-to-face visits, could be effective. The participation of five countries allowed the team to study more than 1,800 suicide attempters and to compare the impact of the intervention to the standard treatment in each setting. At the eighteen-month follow-up stage, just 0.2 percent of those who had received the intervention had died by suicide compared to 2.2 percent of those receiving treatment as usual. Such interventions may work because they promote the social inclusion of people who may otherwise be socially isolated. Participants are also regularly reminded of sources of help, should they experience another suicidal crisis.

Safety-Planning Intervention

The success of interventions involving follow-up contacts relies on a high participation rate by suicide attempters. Unfortunately, many patients do not attend follow-up appointments. This difficulty encouraged Barbara Stanley and Gregory Brown to develop a safety-planning intervention,[10, 11] which they recommend be used in an emergency setting to deliver benefits to people who do not engage in treatment after seeking help.

The safety plan is a structured intervention in the form of a plan developed collaboratively with the patient, but completed in the patient's own words, which the patient will refer to and implement when they face a suicidal crisis. Its use is not restricted to emergency settings, however, and the authors have also adapted it for use by military veterans, children and adolescents. They suggest that it can be used by any person with suicidal ideation or anyone thought to be at a high-risk of suicide, in an inpatient or outpatient setting. The fact that many people expressing suicidal ideation do not have any mental illness means that it can be an effective intervention for those who are at increased risk, but do not require any mental-health care or treatment. For those in treatment, however, Stanley and Brown stress that the plan is just one element of the necessary care package.

The safety plan is wide-ranging and requires a patient to reflect on the different stages of a suicidal crisis and focus on how they will deal with such a crisis at each key point. It involves identifying internal coping strategies, distraction techniques, help-seeking strategies and ways to make the patient's environment safer. The plan consists of six stages, which are to be implemented sequentially – if one step does not alleviate the crisis, the next step should be followed.

1. Recognition of Warning Signs

Firstly, the safety-planning intervention asks each patient to identify the early warning signs that indicate that a suicidal crisis is imminent. If they can identify and pay attention to these triggers, it should be easier for them to avert an impending crisis. Warning signs vary from person to person. They can include negative thought patterns, low mood and behaviours such as drinking excessively.

2. Internal Coping Strategies

Having listed their relevant warning signs, the patient then identifies how they might cope with the situation on their own. With the help of a professional, they are encouraged to think about what they might be able to do before contacting someone. This approach promotes self-reliance and the belief that many crises can be alleviated without outside assistance. Such coping strategies will hopefully distract the patient from their problems, so that thoughts of suicide do not escalate.

Examples of internal coping strategies include listening to music, going for a walk and reading. After the patient identifies some possible coping strategies, it is important for them to discuss each one with the professional. What is the likelihood that they will actually use it? Barriers to employing any strategy should also be discussed. After trouble-shooting any barriers, the patient should have listed a number of activities that they can now use and which they have prioritised based on how easy they will be to implement.

3. Socialisation Strategies for Distraction and Support

Coping strategies implemented by the patient will not always work. When this is the case, the patient should employ strategies that involve mixing with others. It is important to note that this step does not actually involve telling anyone about the suicidal crisis. The feeling of connectedness with other people can serve to distract the patient from suicidal urges and act as a means of support.

Two main types of socialisation strategies are envisaged: mixing with other people and visiting healthy social settings. In the first strategy, the patient will typically visit friends and family members in their homes. In the second, the patient might visit places such as coffee shops, where people socialise naturally. For obvious reasons, bars are excluded.

Once again, a professional should work through this step with the patient and have the patient identify positive social distractors. A priority list of people and settings should be developed so that the patient has other possible options if one of them is unavailable.

4. Social Contacts for Assistance in Resolving Suicidal Crises

If the previous socialisation strategies have not alleviated the crisis, the patient should explicitly inform a trusted friend or family member that they are going through a crisis. The people identified here may have been on the patient's list of people to socialise with in the previous step, but the patient can also identify different people.

The patient must deal head-on with the complex nature of decisions around disclosing suicidal crises to others. The professional must, therefore, discuss the likelihood of the patient contacting each person identified as a possible source of assistance, and specify the advantages and disadvantages of getting in touch with them. If the patient agrees that a particular person would be a help rather than a hindrance, that person should be included.

In a best-case scenario, when the patient is comfortable and consents, the patient will identify someone with whom they can share the plan, who will agree to sign it, signifying that they are acknowledging that the patient has shared it with them and that they accept any tasks allocated to them under this step.

5. Professional and Agency Contacts to Help Resolve Crises

Help-seeking behaviour must sometimes escalate beyond a patient's friends and family, to professionals. The goal of this step of the safety plan is to create a list of professionals, service providers and other organisations that the patient is prepared to contact if they still feel suicidal after going through the previous steps.

Patient fears about disclosure must be recognised, directly dealt with and overcome. The mere mention of professionals and clinicians may lead to fears about being involuntarily detained, for instance. Other barriers to contacting professionals must also be discussed. If a patient does not agree to contact a particular professional or agency in the event of a crisis, they cannot be included.

The list should include the professional or provider's name and contact details. A current mental-health treatment provider should be identified, where this is relevant. Out-of-hours services and other relevant local or national services should also be detailed, where the patient agrees to this.

6. Means Restriction

The final element of the safety plan addresses possible suicide methods. A frank discussion concentrates on the lethal means that the patient might use to kill themself. The professional must then inquire as to whether the patient has a suicide plan involving a specific method.

Even where no such plan is mentioned, steps to limit access to the methods of completing suicide that may be used must still be made. The professional must identify the lethality of any means the patient notes. Where access to an especially lethal method, such as a gun, is noted, the priority of restricting this access increases.

Ideally, this step should involve another person – possibly a friend or relative. This person could store medication safely, for example. The safety plan should list all possible means identified by the patient and the steps to be taken to restrict access for each one.

Afterwards

After the plan has been created, Stanley and Brown offer some final guidance to maximise the likelihood that it will be implemented. They advise the professional to assess the patient's overall reaction to the completed plan. Any aspects that the patient might identify as especially helpful can be highlighted. If the patient indicates an unwillingness to implement some part of the plan, they should work collaboratively with the professional to resolve the issue. The final version should consist entirely of actions that the patient has agreed to implement. The patient is given a copy of the plan, and the patient and professional discuss how it will be accessed in a crisis. Where the safety plan is drawn up in a non-emergency setting, a timescale should be set for it to be reviewed and updated as required.

★

We must be honest and clear that we do not know if the safety-planning intervention prevents suicide. It remains a promising intervention, however, and should at least relieve short-term stress for the suicidal person, his loved ones and the professional.

Crisis services such as those offered by the Samaritans and Pieta House in Ireland are another alternative to the medical model that dominates mental-health services. They take the heat off psychiatric services and are useful interventions that have helped a number of people who have accessed them. Research involving fifty-two clients who used Pieta House services found that following their treatment, they reported significantly higher self-esteem and more reasons for living, as well as significantly lower depression and fewer reasons for dying.[12] Men and women benefitted equally. Of course, none of these findings show though that these services reduce population suicide rates. DBT, lithium and follow-up contacts, which have a solid evidence base behind them, must be prioritised. It would be foolhardy, however, to ignore the value of other services to people in crisis.

13.
Summing Up Suicide Prevention

In Ireland, advocates frequently compare the resources dedicated to preventing deaths from road-traffic accidents with those committed to suicide prevention. They imply that with the right amount of effort and resources, the country could replicate the success it has achieved in reducing deaths from road-traffic accidents, which fell from 472 in 1997 to 190 in 2013.[1] The obvious difference between these two issues is that we do not possess sufficient evidence to know how we might drastically reduce suicide rates. National suicide rates rarely deviate significantly in the short term and in the medium term.

Due to the limited evidence that exists to support existing suicide-prevention initiatives, and because of how different the interventions contained within them are, some suicide experts recommend that what is required is a broad array of suicide-prevention interventions addressing different risk factors at different levels[2] – i.e., the implementation of broad-based suicide-prevention strategies. The logic is essentially this: we do not know what works so we must recommend a range of different initiatives in multiple areas, and maybe some of them will work. A blunderbuss approach, however, is not what we might call a robust platform for establishing effective policy and practice.

Not everyone accepts that all suicide-prevention efforts should be solely evaluated on the basis of evidence. Dr Justin Brophy, chair of the Irish Association of Suicidology, accepts that governments must find evidence for the effectiveness of pro-grammes supported by public money. But that does not mean that programmes that may not merit funding due to a lack of evidence are without value, he argues. Many of these are good in and of themselves, he argues. He points to promoting kindness and compassion for people in distress, which may not immediately save lives from suicide, but is nonetheless positive for society. Philosophically, then, he believes that the benefits of these approaches are defensible pending the availability of definitive evidence supporting their effectiveness in preventing suicide or not.[3]

Dr Brophy's view has some merit and undoubtedly explains the high level of public support for suicide-prevention efforts and the participation of so many people who freely give up their time to take part in voluntary efforts. Dr Dermot Walsh, the former inspector of mental hospitals in Ireland, believes that because suicide is so tragic, the public response to it naturally will be to support any attempt to try and deal with it, even if such an attempt is unwarranted or lacks evidence of effectiveness. He believes that:

> It's all very appropriate in a moral sense but, in a practical sense, you have to ask yourself whether this is a good use of a person's time, a good use of money – and I certainly would ask that question.[4]

Clearly, there is a role for some interventions that currently lack an evidence base, to offer solace to people in crisis. They can assist distressed individuals in developing the problem-solving skills needed to overcome a crisis. Crisis services as offered by the Samaritans and others and interventions such as Brown and Stanley's safety plan are examples of morally appropriate initiatives. What cannot be claimed is that these initiatives reduce population suicide rates. There are also multiple actions in national suicide-prevention strategies that must be financed and resourced and so evidenced-based practices must be prioritised.

A rational examination of the whole area of suicide prevention also means that the term itself is misleading. A number of suicides are inevitable and so, even if evidence-based policies are introduced, the most we can aspire to is to *reduce* suicide numbers. Therefore, if we are going to be honest with ourselves, we should be talking about *suicide-reduction strategies*.

★

What, then, are the implications of the evidence that has been presented in the previous chapters? Certainly, only a few universal approaches, such as means restriction and reducing access to alcohol, have the potential to impact the prevalence of suicide in a country as a whole.

When it comes to means restriction, initiatives such as banning toxic pesticides and introducing restrictive gun laws have very important roles to play, but their likely effectiveness will differ substantially from country to country. How people kill themselves in each country has to be considered, along with the lethality and availability of each method, and the opportunities for restricting it.

When we looked at the different ways that people kill themselves around the world earlier, we observed that pesticides only make a notable contribution to suicide mortality in some countries, such as El Salvador. These countries can achieve dramatic reductions in their overall suicide rates, even if their suicide-prevention efforts focus solely on limiting access to these deadly chemicals. In addition to following Sri Lanka's example by banning the most toxic pesticides, other public-health measures can help reduce the number of deaths they cause. Safely storing these chemicals, ensuring that they are properly disposed of and improving access to aftercare for those who have ingested them are also important.[5] Concerns that agricultural yields would fall or that farming would become more expensive because of new pesticide regulations were shown to be unfounded in the case of Sri Lanka.[6] Many thousands of lives, then, can be saved worldwide if similar restrictions are introduced in other countries.

More than two years after the Sandy Hook elementary school massacre took place in the state of Connecticut in December 2012, no significant changes have been made to gun laws in the USA. There is little cause for optimism. Relatively minor legislative changes such as including mandatory background checks on those seeking to buy firearms failed to win sufficient support in the US Senate. As has usually been the case, the Sandy Hook-inspired gun-control debate failed to focus on the greater potential for guns to be used in suicidal acts than in murders. The message that there is huge scope for suicide numbers to be reduced by making it more difficult for people to access guns needs to be heard more loudly and more consistently. The potential of restricting access to guns to reduce suicides in other countries, besides the USA, also should not be ignored. Guns accounted for more than a third of male suicides and a quarter of female suicides in Argentina between 1997 and 2003, for example.

Seven out of every ten people who hang themselves will die, so this also qualifies as a highly lethal suicide method. Yet, physically restricting access to the means people use to hang themselves may be impossible. Ropes, belts and wires are everyday items with a variety of uses, so there is no straightforward way of preventing vulnerable people from getting their hands on them. In fact, it is likely only possible to restrict access to hanging as a means of suicide in restrictive environments such as inpatient psychiatric facilities and prisons.

Even in countries where guns do not contribute significantly to overall suicide mortality, such as Britain, we know that changes to the law can reduce suicide rates amongst specific groups of the population. For example, changes to gun laws in the UK in 1989 were associated with a fall in the number of suicides amongst farmers.[7] This point is important because, in places such as Britain and Ireland where hanging dominates, pessimism about the potential effectiveness of means restriction is commonplace.

Where the potential for means restriction to significantly reduce national suicide rates is negligible, we should also not dismiss opportunities to lower suicide attempts or numbers of suicide fatalities in a local area. For example, limiting the number of packs of paracetamol that people can purchase in the UK through legislation was not associated with a fall in the overall suicide rate, but it was linked to a decline in the number of suicides involving paracetamol, a decrease in the number of large overdoses involving the drug and a fall in the number of liver transplants required as a result of such overdoses.[8] Other research has shown that restricting access to sites commonly used by people to leap to their deaths is associated with a fall in suicides by jumping and a decline in the suicide rate in the surrounding area.[9, 10, 11]

Though recent experience suggests that substitution to other methods is minimal when access to a means of suicide is restricted, we cannot be sure that this will persist in the longer term. Technological progress may introduce newer ways for people to kill themselves, the media might advertise them and they could become more popular over time.

The experience of the USSR in its final years suggests that introducing restrictions on alcohol can have a dramatic impact on suicide rates, particularly amongst men. However, restrictions as draconian as those implemented by Gorbachev are probably out of the question in most countries. What can be successfully used instead to alter consumption patterns is price.

A comprehensive review (a meta-analysis) carried out in 2009 of 122 studies shows unequivocally that increasing the price of alcohol is the most effective way to reduce harmful drinking.[12] This effect holds true for all types of alcoholic drinks and affects both light drinkers and heavy drinkers. If states are serious about reducing their suicide numbers, such a policy must be given serious consideration. This is especially the case in countries such as Ireland, where 1.35 million people are harmful drinkers and 75 percent of alcohol is consumed in binges.[13]

A bill containing a proposal to place an additional tax on alcohol sold in supermarkets and off-licenses was initiated by Irish senator Marc MacSharry in July 2014. Its purpose was to raise an additional €200 million to fund suicide-prevention programmes including the employment of suicide-prevention resource officers and out-of-hours social-worker teams. This is deeply ironic, since raising the price of alcohol will reduce suicides, but there is no evidence that the suicide-prevention programmes this tax rise is meant to fund will do so.

★

The challenge of reducing the incidence of suicide and suicidal behaviour among those who are at increased risk is different altogether. Mental illness plays a significant role in at least 50 percent of suicides but, in a great many cases, the thesis that mental illness caused a suicide is a convenient fiction. The result of this fiction is to throw a huge degree of responsibility for the prevention of suicide onto mental-health professionals. It has also popularised the notion that prevention of suicide is possible if only mental illnesses could be treated early and effectively enough. Mental-health services have become paralysed by the notion of blame with respect to suicide, to the point that the suicide tail is wagging the dog of the mental-health services.

Good mental-health-care systems still do have a role to play, though. Countries which have high rates of suicide, such as Japan, but invest relatively little in mental-health-care could better tackle their suicide problems by addressing this deficit. Because there are so few interventions that offer the potential to reduce suicide among people with mental illness, clinicians must primarily focus on treating the mental illness, while accepting that some suicides will occur. At the same time, we must not ignore the small number of treatments and interventions that can be used within mental-health services to reduce suicide. The WHO trial involving a brief intervention and follow-up contacts is an important example. It is a relatively low-cost initiative that appears promising for poorer countries, in particular, which wish to cut their suicide numbers but lack the resources to fund other initiatives.

Patients with borderline personality disorder should be offered DBT where this is available. Research involving lithium proves that there is at least one medication that works to reduce suicide among people with depression and bipolar disorders. No one should be treated with DBT or lithium merely to prevent them from killing themself. Their main purpose is to effectively treat the relevant disorder. In the case of lithium, any decision to prescribe it should only be taken after weighing up the advantages and disadvantages associated with it. One counterweight to its many side effects is the demonstrable protective effect that it offers against suicide and its excellent mood-stabilisation properties.

When a suicidal patient no longer requires treatment, they should be discharged. Strategies such as the safety plan and follow-up contacts can then be used as appropriate, and involve family and friends when appropriate. Family members and friends must, however, accept though that many suicides will not be prevented and that mental-health services cannot be relied on to stop these deaths. In hindsight, it might appear that a decision to discharge a loved one from mental-health care or a decision not to admit them was wrong. This is far too simplistic, however, and can lead to the unhelpful blaming of professionals and agencies who will usually have made the best decisions based on the information available to them at the time. Unwarranted admissions or delayed discharges may in themselves increase distress and may deprive other patients with more serious psychiatric conditions of much-needed access to care.

In addition to all of the above, taking a holistic view while acknowledging the evidence vacuum, it is surely the case that a compassionate society is an important foundation for all our specific evidence-based universal suicide-prevention measures. All citizens should be treated fairly and all of us should have access to educational and vocational opportunities as well as good health and mental-health services.

★

As a broad public consensus exists on the merits of preventing suicide, we might expect that implementing those interventions that have been shown to be effective should be relatively straight-forward. Unfortunately, powerful interest groups ensure that this often is not the case. Rene Duignan's campaign to draw attention to the scale of the suicide problem in Japan led to the develop-ment of a very successful documentary film, *Saving 10,000*. It was screened in the Japanese parliament, won awards and was widely distributed on social media. Duignan believes that his ambition to screen the film on mainstream television was thwarted, though, because of some of the industries he links to suicide. These include the drinks industry, which advertises heavily on Japanese television.[14]

In the United States, gun-rights advocates such as the National Rifle Association (NRA) succeeded in removing $2.6 million dedicated to research into gun violence from the budget of the Centers for Disease Control and Prevention in 1996. Tackling the high rate of suicide in the US military has been made more difficult because of a 2010 law promoted by the NRA that prevents army commanders from even asking soldiers who live off base whether they have access to a privately owned weapon.

More than 1,600 people have jumped to their deaths from the Golden Gate Bridge, but efforts to construct a suicide barrier there have long been resisted. Among other reasons, there were concerns that a barrier would visually damage what is universally regarded as a stunning example of human engineering. Finally, though, in June 2014, decades after the campaign for the barrier began, the local highway and transportation district approved a plan to build it. The following month, it was announced that an anti-suicide barrier would be constructed on the George Washington Bridge, which separates New York from New Jersey, from which an average of six people a year jump to their deaths. There is cause for optimism in knowing that battles to implement good suicide-reduction initiatives can take time, but can also eventually succeed.

14.
The Aftermath of a Suicide

Mary Welsh Hemingway's initial decision to lie about how her famous husband died was not unusual. Once suicide survivors start to journey through the bereavement process they usually have to tackle such hurdles as the stigma that surrounds voluntary death. There are no rules which dictate how they must react to these challenges, and hiding the truth is a common reaction. Constant ruminating over 'what ifs' and desperate quests to understand why loved ones chose to die are some of the other typical features of this journey.

Suicide's effects extend beyond families and can ripple through schools, workplaces and entire communities. Lest we forget, doctors, nurses, psychologists and social workers are also human beings. Their roles as health professionals do not prevent them from suffering following the death of a patient. Feelings of guilt and thoughts that they did not do enough to prevent a death are common. These can prompt searching questions around their competence and suitability as caring professionals.

Traditionally, around five or six people were thought to be bereaved by each suicide. However, Norwegian suicide expert Kari Dyregrov believes this figure is too conservative and that a more realistic estimate is between ten and fifteen people.[1] In developing countries, where people have larger family and social networks, it is likely to be larger still. More than 800,000 worldwide suicide fatalities every year means that several million survivors are left behind to cope with the aftermath of these deaths.

The needs of these survivors are the focus of 'postvention' activities. These are initiatives to help grieving relatives and friends in the period after the death. They also incorporate interventions to prevent suicidal behaviour among a group now vulnerable to suicidal impulses. Founded in Ireland in 2002, Console is a suicide-prevention agency that distinguished itself from most others because of the postvention services it offers. These include professional counselling and a liaison service for bereaved families.

The experiences of the families covered in our suicide stories earlier illustrated the many different stages associated with losing someone to suicide. Prior to the death, significant anxiety and stress are typical, especially where there have been previous displays of suicidal behaviour. Sean Quinn and Shane D'Alton had each previously made an attempt on their life. This left their family members constantly on high alert, worrying about further attempts. No-suicide contracts might be made – i.e., promises or deals that the suicidal person will not make another attempt and will get in touch with a loved one if they start to feel down again. Far too often, though, such agreements are not upheld.

The suicide itself is then experienced as deeply traumatic. Discovering the deceased's body or experiencing a visit from the police or a clinician delivering such awful news is unimaginably distressing. Families' hearts are ripped out. The grief is raw. Having to break the news to other family members and facing questions from the police and sympathetic neighbours all take their toll. Then come practicalities, such as having to arrange a funeral.

In Ireland, a suspected suicide must be reported to a coroner. Months later, he will hold a public hearing into the circumstances surrounding the death. If a suicide note was left behind, it may be read out. Details about possible drug and alcohol abuse or relationship difficulties are also sometimes aired. Console is calling for a change to Irish law so that the families of the deceased are not made to feel like they are on trial.

The reality of losing someone to suicide usually stays with people for the rest of their lives. There is, then, a legacy phase that must also be endured, during which it is possible to discover a positive purpose in life.

The Impact of Suicide

Is suicide-related bereavement tougher to deal with than other types of bereavement? Until relatively recently, it was considered to be. And yet, a consensus has now emerged that the grieving process surrounding suicide is not necessarily more difficult than that surrounding deaths from, say, heart disease, accidents or other natural causes.

This is an important message, which can encourage optimism, rather than an assumption that having to cope with a suicide is akin to an insurmountable emotional life sentence. There will, of course, still be many challenges. The risk of developing mental-health difficulties goes up. Pirjo Saarinen and four colleagues confirmed this when they interviewed 104 suicide survivors in Finland and investigated the impacts of these fatalities on the survivors' mental health six months after the deaths. Half of the survivors stated that they needed professional help to cope, yet only a quarter had accessed help.[2] Ten years later, the suicide survivors had experienced more mental-health problems than the general Finnish population.[3]

The important point about suicide-related bereavement, however, is that it is qualitatively different than other forms of grieving. Dr Justin Brophy describes it as:

> an unusual and a ghastly form of pain and suffering . . . that leaves people very marked not just by pain and loss but by guilt, by a sense of complicity, by a sense of doubt, of loss of confidence in their own behaviour, of regret, of enmeshment with . . . a lethal act.[4]

Those bereaved by self-inflicted deaths often confront these fatalities from very different psychological perspectives. Learning of the death of a friend who frequently self-harmed, spent weeks of her life in hospital and seemed to threaten suicide every week may not be unexpected. The suicide of a patient with borderline personality disorder can arrive like death does to the family whose relative has battled for many years through a debilitating cancer. The borderline patient will likely have displayed anger and hostility towards friends and family members, straining relationships and fomenting stress for all involved. As well as not arriving as a shock, such a suicide may even lead to a sense of relief. Relief also usually means guilt. Such a reaction will not apply to most families, though. Even where someone has battled through mental illness for years, their death usually arrives out of the blue.

How an adult adjusts to a suicide can be dramatically different from how a child experiences the suicide of someone who may have been an important role model for them. Just as we speak of many things when we speak of suicide, we must remember that there are many different ways in which families and members of those families are affected by these deaths. Nevertheless, common themes can be identified.

Uneasy Social Relationships

Thankfully, the mass social shunning that characterised communities' reactions to suicide centuries ago has disappeared. That does not mean, though, that all negative social experiences have vanished. Consider a study that compared the experiences of families who lost relatives to suicide to those bereaved from other causes. It found that more than three-quarters (76 percent) of those who had been bereaved following an accidental death reported positive social interactions after the fatality, compared to only one-quarter (27 percent) of those personally affected by suicide.[5] Families reported that significant uncertainty and uneasiness characterised their social interactions. Crucially, families themselves, as well as their friends and social networks, shaped the nature of these interactions.

Decisions to keep the nature of a suicide death a secret are sometimes taken by families, of course. Negative reactions from others are, unfortunately, all too real. People may go out of their way to avoid talking to the deceased's family – perhaps deliberately crossing the street. Others may make thoughtless remarks or completely avoid the subject of the death. In extreme cases, some might blame the family for the death. Such hostile reactions are directed especially at the parents of a child who has taken their own life.[6]

We may be conveying the impression that compassion and support are hardly ever offered to suicide survivors. People are not that heartless. Much needed support is, in fact, regularly made available and appreciated. Families report, though, that they need support for a long time, but it often diminishes after a relatively short time. Even when compassion and support are on offer, survivors may practice a form of 'self-stigmatisation', in which they retreat from support or avoid other people.[7]

Making Sense of the Suicide

How do you make sense of a suicide? Inevitably, much effort is expended in a quest to understand why the deceased felt they had no other option other than to take their own life, even though the quest will usually be fruitless and unhelpful.

The absence of straightforward answers can torture people. Also torturous are the variety of negative emotions that can be experienced in the aftermath of a voluntary death. Shame and loss of trust are common. A realisation that only acute distress would have led the deceased to take their own life can prompt horror among loved ones at their inability to recognise it and intervene. Another burden is guilt because they did not recognise that their loved one was in imminent danger or do enough to prevent their death. How unfortunate it is, then, that an understanding that skilled mental-health professionals are themselves unable to predict who is likely to kill themself is not more widely known. Such information can clearly help loved ones to stop blaming themselves. Trying to make meaning of the death also entails struggles with other questions. Why was the deceased unable, for example, to confide the true nature of their problems?

Anger at the suicide victim is normal, although suicide survivors often feel guilty about it and have difficulty admitting to it. They are angry because they feel they have been abandoned and rejected and because of the devastating impact that the suicide has unleashed. Anger can also be directed at health professionals and mental-health services for not doing more to prevent the death. The belief that the death should have been prevented by professionals can escalate, on occasion, to claims of malpractice being filed against clinicians. Usually, such anger and allocation of blame is misplaced. Fear about the impact of the suicide on the wider family often leaves people haunted by the worry that other family members may kill themselves. Keeping a close eye over them is common.

This range of negative emotions is completely normal and natural. Those who have lost someone to suicide should be reminded of this regularly.

In the midst of the darkness associated with suicide, we should stress that the bereaved can find positive meanings from the trauma they have gone through. Many survivors identify a new purpose in their lives. They want to help others and to prevent other suicides. Phyllis McNamara, whose husband Michael took his own life, describes this purpose as a vocation.

Health Professionals

As most concern is understandably focussed on the family of the deceased following a suicide, it can easily be forgotten that health professionals may suffer and grieve too. Breaking the news of a death to a family is tough in any circumstances, but when you are aware that they may blame you for the death, it is tougher still. Three out of ten German psychiatrists and psychologists who had experienced a patient's suicide reported that they suffered from severe distress.[8]

Consultant psychiatrist Declan Murray has described dealing with the aftermath of a suicide as a nightmare – the worst thing that he has had to do as a health professional.[9] Dr Justin Brophy knows clinicians who have been traumatised by such deaths. They can become 'super defensive, suspicious, wary, unable to deal with risk, withdrawn and very damaged', he says.[10] Brophy believes, though, that dealing with suicides is a professional burden that must be borne. All practitioners must reflect and learn and adapt their professional response, which can ultimately prove to be a very rich – as well as a very painful – journey.[11]

Clinicians find that they can experience negative emotions similar to those experienced by family members. These include denial, disbelief, anger and guilt. Social workers who have experienced suicides have said: 'It makes me question being in the field when that happens. It makes me feel like I don't know what the hell I'm doing and that I have no business being a therapist,'[12] and '[I was] a total failure as a therapist. How could I not save him? I felt I failed the family.'[13] Health professionals need to be reminded of the complexity of suicide and of how difficult it is to predict.

As well as normalising the experience of emotions such as relief and anger at the deceased, what else might suicide survivors do to deal with the death? Moving on from trying to understand why it happened undoubtedly helps. Survivors should also seek out suicide-bereavement support groups. The WHO reports that there has been a welcome expansion of such groups worldwide since 2000. However, they are still only available in 42 percent of countries. This is disappointing, because we know they can be very effective in helping the bereaved to overcome their distress. They should be rapidly expanded worldwide, and all those living in countries where they are available should be encouraged to attend them.

15.
Adding It All Up

Suicide occurs within every country and culture. All available evidence suggests that this has been the case throughout human history. The ancient Greeks and Romans did not shy away from discussing it. The stories of famous and heroic suicides from the period, such as those of Ajax and Lucretia, still captivated minds centuries later. Renaissance artists portrayed their deaths sympathetically, and Shakespeare and others wrote plays and poems about them. As a result, if you were well off and literate, it was sometimes possible, even during the height of Christian intolerance towards suicide, to access alternative and less-hostile depictions of suicide. So dominant was Christianity's position in the Western world for more than a millennium, however, and so acute was its hostility towards voluntary death, that any frank discussion of the topic was usually off limits.

Only in the nineteenth century, when it became more acceptable to show compassion towards suicidal individuals, did we begin to see suicide investigated using modern scientific approaches. This allowed us to discover more about the issue. Many suicide victims endure intense heartache and suffering before their deaths, often over a sustained period. Rarely is such distress linked to a single vulnerability. Comic genius Robin

Williams struggled with depression before ending his life. But he also had a history of drug and alcohol abuse and had been recently diagnosed with Parkinson's disease.

We also know that there are many people who act on suicidal impulses, within relatively short periods of time. Often, less than five minutes elapse before someone acts on a decision to die. At an aggregate level, we know that the prevalence of suicide is influenced by the economic situation in a country, the availability of lethal means of self-injury and the media's coverage of celebrity suicides. Suicide's complexity, its multiple causes and its unpredictability are just some of the challenges that those wishing to prevent it must confront.

Suicide leaves behind a trail of grief in its aftermath that can shock and numb families and friends to the core. Some people never fully recover from losing someone to such a death. Tragically, suicide's copycat effect means that a single fatality can spark a chain reaction of further deaths among grieving relatives and friends.

While in-depth investigation of the subject has helped us to understand more about suicide, there is much that we still do not know. Why does Ireland have an especially high rate of suicide among young men, for example? Why are Irish people almost twice as likely as Britons to kill themselves? Why has suicide increased so dramatically in South Korea in recent years? We can only provide partial or inconclusive answers to such questions. Many individual cases of suicide also have no obvious causes.

That there are so many unanswered questions probably explains why suicide is so misunderstood among the public. Common myths include linking suicide almost exclusively to mental illness. Though it is an important factor, there is a significant minority of suicides in which it plays no role, and there are others in which it is only a minor contributory factor. Public assumptions that mental-health services should be relied upon to prevent suicide are also misguided. As a result, people who are not mentally ill are frequently and inappropriately hospitalised. Society as a whole is also over-estimating the risk of suicide. Though suicidal thoughts are relatively common, suicide itself is very rare. Its tragic nature means that the attention focussed on the problem is disproportionally large compared to its statistical frequency.

Suicide's tragic aspects must be acknowledged, but there is also a need to recognise the rights of the individual to liberty and autonomy. This will sometimes mean that a person's decision to end his life cannot be condemned. Most suicides should, however, be discouraged; we should try to reduce the number of people who die this way.

And yet, aside from a few exceptions, the quest to find a solution to the problem of suicide has been especially disappointing. To claim, as the World Health Organization recently has, that suicides are preventable is a little misleading. Certainly, some suicides can be prevented and there are a number of public-health interventions which, if implemented, can reduce population suicide rates. Suicide attempts and rates of self-harm can also be reduced by employing these and a limited number of other interventions.

However, although we are strong and successful as a species, individual humans are frail and imperfect and some will always choose to exit life when confronted with predicaments. The self-preservation instinct that has enabled humans to thrive belongs on a spectrum. Some people clearly cling to life more tenaciously than others. In individual cases, we must be honest and state that while we can provide useful care and solace to many people in crisis, we must expect that some of them will go on to kill themselves. Not all suicides are preventable and there are no foolproof measures that we can adopt that will ensure that a person deemed to be low-risk or someone deemed to be high-risk will not go on to end their life.

The friends and family members of a suicide victim may assume that a suicide could and should have been prevented. They may blame themselves or others for the fatality. Not only are such beliefs often wrong, they can hinder the friends and family members' efforts to come to terms with the death and make the bereavement process more difficult.

Because suicide is so tragic, because it is so misunderstood and especially because so many young men die from suicide in Ireland, the equivalent of a moral panic has spread over the land, leading to the mushrooming of suicide-prevention agencies and other initiatives. What was once a taboo is now discussed openly and journalists are reflecting public interest in the topic by covering the subject in great detail.[*] Sometimes, tragic suicides are sensationally covered and, across the world, journalists focus on suicide methods that are not at all representative of how people actually die.

But we must be mindful that suicide ought to be discouraged and that excess publicity regarding suicide and suicide risk may be making the whole notion more acceptable. The state should be especially careful not to legitimise suicidal behaviour as a normal response to stressful circumstances. Our discussion of Ireland's recent abortion legislation, the Protection of Life During Pregnancy Act 2013, argued that the Irish state has done just this by passing a law that lacks an evidence base.

Even well-intentioned initiatives such as media campaigns around World Suicide-Prevention Day or publicised fundraising initiatives to combat suicide may not be helpful. We are told that we need to talk more about suicide and yet the terms of suicidality are part of the everyday argot, especially among young people. Just as suicide leads to more suicides, the consequences of using these words may be making more individuals act in this manner.

Philosopher Jennifer Hecht has argued that we need to discourage suicide, pointing out that it is wrong and that it harms the community. She is right to suggest that maintaining a taboo around taking one's life can be helpful. We believe this is not at odds with the admirable efforts to destigmatise mental ill-health and help-seeking behaviour; people should, of course, be aware of sources of help when they face a crisis. However, Hecht's suggestion that anti-suicide sentiments be actively disseminated may be counterproductive, possibly focussing even more attention on an issue that already has no shortage of publicists. Society needs to become less obsessed with suicide and suicidal behaviour and instead address it in a calm, rational, evidence-informed way.

A rational approach to tackling the problem of suicide would involve putting in place humane measures which can reduce suicide rates and improve the lives of individuals in the longer term. We must, however, recognise that suicide is part of the human condition. The proper aim, then, should be to mitigate its harmful effects and create a society where the experience of despair will be minimised, and where people will have the opportunity to live productive and fulfilled lives.

*This book may be regarded as an example of this.

Notes

Chapter One | Introduction

1. Harris, A. 'No Shame in Feeling Despair'. *Irish Times* online, 8 September 2014 (cited 5 October 2014). Available from irishtimes.com/life-and-style/health-family/no-shame-in-feeling-despair-1.1916755 2014.

2. The Oxford English Dictionary defines obsession as an idea or thought that continually preoccupies or intrudes on a person's mind.

3. Anderson, O. *Suicide in Victorian and Edwardian England*. Oxford: Oxford University Press, 1987.

4. Szasz, T. *Fatal Freedom: The Ethics and Politics of Suicide*. Syracuse: Syracuse University Press, 1999.

5. Brophy, J. Interviewed by Beattie, D. on 25 March 2014.

6. Emile Durkheim. *Suicide: A Study in Sociology*. New York: The Free Press, 1897 (1951), p54.

7. Quoted in Schwartz, B. *The Paradox of Choice: Why More Is Less*. New York: Harper, 2004, p42.

8. Hames, J.L., Ribeiro, J.D., Smith, A.R. and Joiner, T.E. 'An urge to jump affirms the urge to live: An empirical examination of the high place phenomenon. In Journal of Affective Disorders. 2012; 136 (3): pp. 1114 - 1120.

Chapter Two | Suicide: A Brief History

1. Livius, Titus. *Ab Urbe Condita*. Book 1, sections 57-60; and Dionysius of Halicarnassus. Ernest Cary (translator), William Thayer (editor). *Roman Antiquities*, Book IV, sections 64-85. Loeb Classical Library. Cambridge, MA: Harvard University. 1939 (2007).

2. Van Hooff, A. 'A Historical Perspective on Suicide'. In Maris, R.W., Berman, A.L. and Silverman, M.M. (editors). *Comprehensive Textbook of Suicidology*. Oxford: Guilford Press, 2000.

3. Van Hooff, A, *From Authonasia to Suicide: Self-Killing in Classical Antiquity*. London: Routledge, 1990.

4. De Roisin, F. *Franchises, Lois et Coutumes de la Ville de Lille*, 1844. Cited in Murray, A. *Suicide in the Middle Ages. Volume 1: The Violence Against Themselves*. Oxford: Oxford University Press, 1998, p28.

5. MacDonald, M. and Murphy, T.R. *Sleepless Souls: Suicide in Early Modern England*. Oxford: Clarendon Press, 1993; and Walsh, D. *Suicide, Attempted Suicide and Prevention in Ireland and Elsewhere*. Dublin: HRB, 2006.

6. Pinguet, M. *Voluntary Death in Japan*. Cambridge: Polity, 1993.

7. Axell, A. and Kase, H. *Kamikaze: Japan's Suicide Gods*. Harlow: Longman, 2002.

8. Szasz, T. *Fatal Freedom: The Ethics and Politics of Suicide*. Syracuse: Syracuse University Press, 1999.

9. Quoted in Pinguet, M. 1993, pp1-2.

10. Van Hooff, A. 2000, p98.

11. Plato. Bury, R.G. (translator). *The Laws*. New York: G.P. Putnam's Sons, 1926.

12. Alvarez, A. *The Savage God*. London: Random House, 1970.

13. Augustine of Hippo. *City of God*. Book 1, c19.

14. Quoted in Murray, A. *Suicide in the Middle Ages. Volume 2: The Curse on Self-Murder*. Oxford: Oxford University Press, 1998, p16.

15. Murray, A. 1998.

16. Murray, A. 1998.

17. Hecht, J.M. *Stay: A History of Suicide and the Philosophies Against It*. London: Yale University Press, 2013.

18. Hume, D. 'Essay 1'. In *Essays on Suicide*, 1783, pp20-21.

19. Anderson, O. 1987.

20. Kichinosuke Tatai. 'Japan'. In Headley, L.A. (editor). *Suicide in Asia and the Near East*. London: University of California Press, 1983.

21. Van Hooff, A. 1990.

22. Alvarez, A. 1970.

23. Anderson, O. 1987.

24. Anderson, O. 1987.

25. Anderson, O. 1987.

26. Anderson, O. 1987.

Chapter Three | Answering Key Suicide Questions: Why? What?

1. World Health Organization. 'Preventing Suicide: A Global Imperative'. Geneva: WHO, 2014.

2. Yang, G.H., Phillips, M.R., Zhou, M.G., Wang, L.J., Zhang, Y.P. and Xu, D. 'Understanding the Unique Characteristics of Suicide in China: National Psychological Autopsy Study'. In *Biomedical and Environmental Sciences*. 2005; 18: pp379-89;

and Manoranjitham, S., Rajkumar, A., Thangadurai, P., Prasad, J., Jayakaran, R. and Jacob, K.S. 'Risk Factors for Suicide in Rural South India', in *British Journal of Psychiatry*. 2010; 196: pp26-30; and Zhang, J., Xiao, S. and Zhou, L. 'Mental Disorders and Suicide Among Young Rural Chinese: A Case-control Psychological Autopsy Study'. In *American Journal of Psychiatry*. 2010; 167: pp773-781; and Pridmore, S. *Suicide and Predicament: Life Is a Predicament*. Bentham Science Publishers, 2010.

3. Arensman, E. Interviewed by Beattie, D. on 26 July 2013.

4. Brent, D and Melhem, N. 'Familial Transmission of Suicidal Behaviour'. In *Psychiatric Clinics of North America*. 2008; 31: pp157-177; and Pridmore. 2010.

5. Duignan, R. Interviewed by Beattie, D. 22 November 2013.

6. Arensman, E., McAuliffe, C., Corcoran, P., Williamson, E., O'Shea, E. and Perry, I.J. 'First Report of the Suicide Information System'. Cork: National Suicide Research Foundation, 2012.

7. Quoted in Frend, T. 'Jumpers: The Fatal Grandeur of the Golden Gate Bridge'. *New Yorker* (online). 13 October 2003 (cited 5 February 2014). Available from www.newyorker.com/archive/2003/10/13/031013fa_fact?currentPage=all.

8. Quoted in Kedmey, D. 'Vatican Official Calls Britany Maynard's Assisted Suicide Reprehensible'. *Time* (online). 4 November 2014 (cited 9 November 2014). Available from time.com/3557113/vatican-official-condemns-brittany-may-nard-death/.

9. Quoted in Kedmey, D. 2014.

10. Murphy, N. 'Lack of Religion Linked to Teen Depression'. *Irish Examiner* (online). 4 November 2014 (cited 6 November

2014). Available from irishexaminer.com/ireland/lack-of-religion-linked-to-teen-depression-296227.html.

11. Kleiman, E.M. and Liu, R.T. 'Prospective Prediction of Suicide in a Nationally Representative Sample: Religious Service Attendance as a Protective Factor'. In *British Journal of Psychiatry*. 2014; 204: pp262-266.

12. Corcoran, P. and Nagar, A. 'Suicide and Marital Status in Northern Ireland'. In *Social Psychiatry and Psychiatric Epidemiology*. 2009; 45: pp795-800.

13. Pridmore. 2010.

14. Casey, P., Dunn, G., Kelly, B.D., Lehtinen, V., Dalgard, O.S., Dowrick, C. et al. 'The Prevalence of Suicidal Ideation in the General Population: Results from the Outcome of Depression International Network (ODIN) Study'. In *Social Psychiatry and Psychiatric Epidemiology*. 2008; 43: pp299-304.

15. National Suicide Research Foundation. 'National Registry of Deliberate Self-Harm Ireland Annual Report'. Cork: NSRF, 2013.

16. St Patrick's University Hospital Written Submission. In *Houses of the Oireachtas Joint Committee on Health and Children: Report on Public Hearings on the Implementation of the Government Decision Following the Publication of the Expert Group Report on A, B, & C vs Ireland, Vol. 2*. Dublin: Houses of the Oireachtas, p394.

Chapter Four | Answering Other Key Suicide Questions

1. World Health Organization. 'Preventing Suicide: A Global Imperative'. Geneva: WHO, 2014.

2. Varnik, P. 'Suicide in the World'. In *International Journal of Environmental Research and Public Health*. 2012; 9: pp760-771.

3. Phillips, M.R., Li, X and Zhang, Y. 'Suicide Rates in China,

1995-99'. In *The Lancet*, 2002; 359 (9309): pp835-40.

4. Savill, R. 'Chemist Used Plant to Commit Suicide'. *Telegraph* (online). 6 October 2006 (cited 7 March 2014). Available from www.telegraph.co.uk/news/1530689/Chemist-used-plant-to-commit-suicide.html.

5. Van Hooff, A. *From Authonasia to Suicide: Self-Killing in Classical Antiquity*. London: Routledge; 1990, pp65-67.

6. Freeman, J. Interviewed by Beattie, D. 7 August 2013.

7. Arensman, E. Interviewed by Beattie, D. 26 July 2013.

8. Freeman, J. 2013.

9. Weiyuan, C. 'Women and Suicide in Rural China'. *Bulletin of the World Health Organization* (online). December 2009 (cited 15 July 2014); 87 (12): pp885-964. Available from www.who.int/bulletin/volumes/87/12/09-011209/en/.

10. Connolly, J.F., Cullen, A., Walsh, D., McGauran, S and Phelan, D. 'A Comparison of Suicide in Two Irish Counties'. In *Irish Journal of Psychological Medicine*. 1999; 16 (4): pp136-39.

Chapter Five | Misunderstanding Suicide, a Case Study: Ireland's Abortion Legislation

1. Human Rights Watch. 'A State of Isolation: Access to Abortion for Women in Ireland'. New York: HRW, 2010.

2. Irish Family Planning Association. Statistics. IFPA (online). Publication date unavailable. (Cited 2 April 2014). Available from www.ifpa.ie/Hot-Topics/Abortion/Statistics.

3. Centre for Maternal and Child Enquiries. 'Saving Mothers' Lives: Reviewing Maternal Deaths to Make Motherhood Safer: 2006-08. The Eighth Report on Confidential Enquiries into Maternal Deaths in the United Kingdom'. In *BJOG, An*

International Journal of Obstetrics and Gynaecology. 2011; 118 (Suppl. 1): pp1-203.

4. Amnesty International Ireland. 'Ireland's New Abortion Guidelines Endanger the Lives and Rights of Women and Girls'. Dublin: Amnesty International Ireland (online), 19 September 2014 (cited 1 November 2014). Available from www.amnesty.ie/news/ireland%E2%80%99s-new-abortion-guidelines-endanger-lives-and-rights-women-and-girls.

5. Academy of Medical Royal Colleges and National Collaborating Centre for Mental Health. 'Induced Abortion and Mental Health: A Systematic Review of the Mental Health Outcomes of Induced Abortion, Including their Prevalence and Associated Factors'. London: NCCMH, 2011.

6. Irish Family Planning Association. Written Submission by the Irish Family Planning Association. In *Houses of the Oireachtas Joint Committee on Health and Children, Vol. 1,* 2013, p138.

7. O'Mahoney, R. Presentation to the Joint Committee on Health and Children. 'Report on Public Hearings on the Implementation of the Government Decision Following the Publication of the Expert Group Report on A, B, & C vs Ireland'. In *Houses of the Oireachtas Joint Committee on Health and Children*, 2013, pp90-96.

8. Bourke, J. *Dismembering the Male: Men's Bodies, Britain and the Great War*. London: Reaktion Books, 1996; and Wessely, S'. Malingering: Historical Perspectives'. In Halligan, P.W., Bass, C. and Oakley, D.A. (editors). *Malingering and Illness Deception*. Oxford University Press, 2003, pp31-41.

9. Sulzbach, W. *German Experience with Social Insurance*. New York: National Industrial Conference Board, 1947; and

Halligan, P.W., Bass, C. and Oakley, D.A. 'Wilful Deception as Illness Behaviour'. In Halligan, P.W., Bass C. and Oakley, D.A. (editors), 2003, pp3-30.

10. Abortion Act, United Kingdom. 1867 (cited 5 October 2014). Available from www.legislation.gov.uk/ukpga/1967/87/contents.

11. British Pregnancy Advisory Service. Newsletter. May 2012. Cited in Casey, P. 'Suicide in Pregnancy and Abortion: Considering the Expert Group Report to the ABC Ruling by the ECHR'. In *Houses of the Oireachtas Joint Committee on Health and Children, Vol. 1*, 2013, pp109-123.

Chapter Six | Suicide Stories

1. Reng, R. *Robert Enke: A Life Too Short*. London: Random House, 2012.

2. O'Brien, C. 'Stories of Suicide'. *Irish Times*. 13 November 2010, pp13-19.

3. Reng, R. 2012. p199.

4. Reng, R. 2012. p376.

5. Martin, C.D. 'Ernest Hemingway: The Psychological Autopsy of a Suicide'. In *Psychiatry*. 2006; 69(4): pp351-61.

6. Lynn, K.S. *Hemingway*. New York: Simon & Schuster, 1987; and Martin. 2006.

7. Quoted in O'Brien, C. 'Stories of Suicide'. *Irish Times*. 15 November 2010.

8. Ibid.

9. Quoted in O'Brien, C. 'Stories of Suicide'. *Irish Times*. 17 November 2010.

10. Quoted in O'Brien, C. 'Stories of Suicide'. *Irish Times*. 13 November 2010.

11. Quoted in O'Brien, C. 'Stories of Suicide'. *Irish Times.* 13 November 2010.

12. Freeman, J. Interviewed by Beattie, D. 7 August 2013.

Chapter Seven | Suicide and the Economy

1. Eurostat. Unemployment Statistics. 2014 (cited 5 April 2014). Available from epp.eurostat.ec.europa.eu/statistics_explained/index.php/Unemployment_statistics#Notes.

2. Eurostat. Unemployment Statistics. 2014 (cited 5 April 2014). Available from epp.eurostat.ec.europa.eu/statistics_explained/index.php/Unemployment_statistics#Notes.

3. Quoted in Stuckler, D., Basu, S., Suhrcke, M., Coutts, A., McKee, M. 'The Public Health Effect of Economic Crises and Alternative Policy Responses in Europe: An Empirical Analysis'. In *The Lancet.* 2009; 374 (9686): pp315-323.

4. Sainsbury, P., Jenkins, J. and Levey, A. 'The Social Correlates of Suicide in Europe'. In Farmer M (editor). *Suicide Syndrome.* London: Croom and Helm, 1980; and Stack, S. 'Work and the Economy'. In Maris, R.W., Berman, A.L. and Silverman, M.M. (editors). *Comprehensive Textbook of Suicidology.* Oxford: Guilford Press, 2000, pp193-221.

5. Luo, F, Florence, C.S., Quispe-Agnoli, M., Ouyang, L. and Crosby, A.E. 'Impact of Business Cycles on US Suicide Rates, 1928–2007'. In *American Journal of Public Health.* 2011; 101 (6): pp1139-1146.

6. Wada, K., Kondo, N., Gilmour, S., Ichida, Y., Fujino, Y., Satah, T. et al. 'Trends in Cause-Specific Mortality Across Occupations in Japanese Men of Working Age During a Period of Economic Stagnation, 1980-2005: Retrospective Cohort Study'. In *British Medical Journal.* 2012; 344 (e1191).

7. McCoy, T. 'Fukushima Aftermath, Suicides Soar'. *Washington Post*. 13 March 2014 (cited 2 June 2014). Available from www.washingtonpost.com/news/morning-mix/wp/2014/03/13/in-fukushima-aftermath-suicides-soar.

8. Duignan, R. Interviewed by Beattie, D. 22 November 2013.

9. Lewis, G and Sloggett, A. 'Suicide, Deprivation, and Unemployment: Record Linkage Study'. In *British Medical Journal*. 1998; 317: pp1283-1286.

10. Ruhm, C.J. 'Good Times Make You Sick'. In *Journal of Health Economics*. 2003; 22: pp637-658.

11. Gerdtham, U.G. and Ruhm, C.J. 'Deaths Rise in Good Economic Times: Evidence from the OECD'. In *Economics and Human Biology*. 2006; 4: pp298-316.

12. Tapia Granados, J.A. and Ionides, E.L. 'The Reversal of the Relation Between Economic Growth and Health Progress: Sweden in the 19th and 20th Centuries'. In *Journal of Health Economics*. 2008; 27: pp544-563.

13. Chang, S.S., Gunnell, D., Sterne, J.A.C., Lu, T.H. and Cheng, A.T.A. 'Was the Economic Crisis 1997-1998 Responsible for Rising Suicide Rates in East/Southeast Asia? A Time-trend Analysis for Japan, Hong Kong, South Korea, Taiwan, Singapore and Thailand'. In *Social Science & Medicine*. 2009; 68: pp1322–1331.

14. Stuckler, D., Basu, S., Suhrcke, M., Coutts, A. and McKee, M. 'The Public-health Effect of Economic Crises and Alternative Policy Responses in Europe: An Empirical Analysis'. In *The Lancet*. 2009; 374: pp315-23.

Chapter Eight | Suicide and the Modern Media: Are We Doing More Harm than Good?

1. Sisask, M. and Varnik, A. 'Media Roles in Suicide Prevention: A Systematic Review'. In *International Journal of Environmental Research and Public Health*. 2012; 9: pp123-138.

2. Fu, K.W. and Yip, P.S.F. 'Estimating the Risk for Suicide Following the Suicide Deaths of Three Asian Celebrities: A Meta-Analytic Approach'. In *Journal of Clinical Psychiatry*. 2009; 70 (6): pp869-878.

3. Sisask, M. and Varnik, A. 2012.

4. Phillips, B., Ball, C., Sackett, D., Badenoch, D., Straus, S., Haynes, B. et al (updated by Howick, J.). 'Oxford Centre for Evidence-Based Medicine – Levels of Evidence'. November 1998 (updated March 2009, cited 1 February 2015). Available from www.cebm.net/oxford-centre-evidence-based-medicine-levels-evidence-march-2009.

5. Phillips, D. 'The Influence of Suggestion on Suicide: Substantial and Theoretical Implications of the Werther Effect'. In *American Sociological Review*. 1974; 39: pp340-354; and Maris, R.W., Berman, A.L. and Silverman, M.M. 'The Social Relations of Suicide'. In Maris, R.W., Berman, A.L. and Silverman, M.M. (editors). Comprehensive *Textbook of Suicidology*. Oxford: Guilford Press, 2000, pp240-65.

6. Pirkis, J., Blood, R.W., Francis, C. and McCallum, K.. 'A Review of the Literature Regarding Film and Television Drama Portrayals of Suicide'. University of Melbourne Program Evaluation Unit, 2005.

7. Ellis, S.J. and Walsh, M.T. 'Soap May Seriously Damage Your Health'. In *The Lancet*. 1986; 327 (8482) 686; and Pirkis, J., Blood, R.W., Francis, C. and McCallum, K. 2005.

8. Sandler, D.A., Connell, P.A. and Welsh, K. 'Emotional Crises Imitating Television'. In *The Lancet*. 1986; 327 (8485): 856; and Pirkis, J., Blood, R.W., Francis, C. and McCallum, K. 2005.

9. Fowler, B.P. 'Emotional Crises Imitating Television'. In *The Lancet*. 1986; 327 (8488): pp1036-1037; and Pirkis, J., Blood, R.W., Francis, C. and McCallum, K. 2005.

10. Williams, J.M., Lawton, C., Ellis, S.J., Walsh, S. and Reed, J. 'Copycat Suicide Attempts'. In *The Lancet*. 330 (8550): pp102-103; and Pirkis, J., Blood, R.W., Francis, C. and McCallum, K. 2005.

11. Platt, S. 'The Aftermath of Angie's Overdose: Is Soap (Opera) Damaging to Your Health?' In *British Medical Journal Clinical Research Edition*. 1987; 294 (6577): 954-957; and Pirkis, J., Blood, R.W., Francis, C. and McCallum, K. 2005.

12. Pirkis, J., Blood, R.W., Francis, C. and McCallum K. 2005.

13. World Health Organization and International Association for Suicide Prevention. 'Preventing Suicide: A Resource for Media Professionals'. Geneva: WHO, 2008.

14. Phillips, D.P., Carstensen, L. and Paight, D. 'Effects of Mass Media News Stories on Suicide with New Evidence on Story Content'. In Peiffer, Cynthia (editor). *Suicide Among Youth: Perspectives on Risk & Prevention*. Washington, DC: American Psychiatric Press, 1989, pp101-116.

15. Goldney, R. 'Suicide: The Role of the Media'. In *Australian and New Zealand Journal of Psychiatry*. 1989 23 (1), pp30-34.

16. Quoted in O'Shea, J. 'Critics of Dead Irish Government Minister Called "Faceless Cowards"'. *Irish Central* (online). 25 December 2012 (cited 7 September 2014). Available from irishcentral.com/news/critics-of-dead-irish-government-minister-called-faceless-cowards-184733161-237555281.html.

Chapter Nine | The Rights and Wrongs of Suicide

1. Condon, D. 'McDaid Apologises for Suicide Comments'. *Irish Health* (online). 1 May 2002 (cited 26 May 2014). Available from www.irishhealth.com/article.html?id=3803.

2. Glennon, C. 'Embattled McDaid Sorry for "Selfish Suicide Jibe"'. *Irish Independent* (online). 1 May 2002 (cited 26 May 2014). Available from independent.ie/national-news/embat-tled-mcdaid-sorry-for-selfish-suicide-jibe-304861.html.

3. Quoted in Fairbairn, G. *Contemplating Suicide: The Language and Ethics of Self-Harm*. London: Routledge, 1995.

4. Duignan, R. Interviewed by Beattie, D. 22 November 2013.

5. Gauthier, S., Mausbach, J., Reisch, T. and Bartsch, C. 'Suicide Tourism: A Pilot Study on the Swiss Phenomenon'. In *Journal of Medical Ethics* (online). 20 August 2014.

6. Hecht, J.M. *Stay: A History of Suicide and the Philosophies Against It*. London: Yale University Press, 2013, p11.

7. Emile Durkheim. *Suicide: A Study in Sociology*. New York: The Free Press, 1897 (1951), p54.

8. Oxford Dictionary of English (online), 7 August 2014. Available from oxforddictionaries.com.

9. Oxford Dictionary of English (online), 7 August 2014. Available from oxforddictionaries.com.

10. Quoted in Wood, K. 'High Court Refuses to Grant Right to Die'. *Sunday Business Post* (online). 10 January 2013 (cited 27 May 2014). Available from businesspost.ie/#!story/Home/News/High+Court+refuses+to+grant+right+to+die/id/1941 0615-5218-50ee-fa6c-e04af8619798.

11. Quoted in Wood, K. 'Ban Protects the Vulnerable, Says Court'. *Irish Examiner* (online). 11 January 2013 (cited 27

May 2014). Available from irishexaminer.com/archives/2013/0111/ireland/ban-protects-the-vulnerable-says-court-219269.html.

12. Battin, M.P. *Ethics and the Way We Die*. Oxford: Oxford University Press, 2005, p20.

13. Humphry, D. *Final Exit: The Practicalities of Self-deliverance and Assisted Suicide for the Dying* (Third Edition). New York: Dell, 2002.

14. Marzuk, P.M., Tardiff, K., Hirsch, C.S., Leon, A.C., Stajic, M., Hartwell, N et al. 'Increase in Suicide by Asphyxiation in New York City After the Publication of Final Exit'. In *The New England Journal of Medicine*. 1993; 329(20): pp1508-1510.

15. Arensman, E. Interviewed by Beattie, D. 26 July 2013.

16. Quoted in James L. Werth Jr. *Rational Suicide? Implications for Mental Health Professionals*. Oxford: Taylor and Francis, 1996.

17. Werth Jr, J.L. 1996.

18. Fairbairn, G. 1995.

Chapter Ten | Introduction to Suicide Prevention

1. Seiden, R. 'Where Are They Now? A Follow-up Study of Suicide Attempters from the Golden Gate Bridge'. In *Suicide and Life-Threatening Behaviour*. 1978; 8 (4): pp203-216.

2. Scott, A. and Guo, B. 'For Which Strategies of Suicide Prevention Is There Evidence of Effectiveness?' Copenhagen: WHO Regional Office for Europe: Health Evidence Network Report, 2012, p15.

3. Mann, J.J., Apter, A., Bertolote, J., Beautrais, A., Currier, D., Hass, A. et al. 'Suicide-Prevention Strategies: A Systematic Review'. In *Journal of the American Medical Association*. 2005; 291 (16): pp2064-2074.

4. Nordentoft, M. 'Crucial Elements in Suicide Prevention Strategies'. In *Progress in Neuro-psychopharmacology and Biological Psychiatry*. 2011; 35: pp848-53.

Chapter Eleven: Suicide Prevention | What Works? Universal Preventative Measures

1. Quoted in Poland, S. *Suicide Prevention in the Schools*. Oxford: Guilford Press, 1989, p163.

2. Plath, S. *The Bell Jar*. London: Faber, 1963 (1996), p131.

3. Clarke, R.V. and Mayhew, P. 'Crime as Opportunity: A Note on Domestic-Gas Suicide in Britain and the Netherlands'. In *British Journal of Criminology, Delinquency and Deviant Social Behaviour*. 1989; 29 (1): p35.

4. Gunnell, D., Fernando, R., Hewagama, M., Priyangika, W.D.D., Konradsen, F. and Eddlestone, M. 'The Impact of Pesticide Regulations on Suicide in Sri Lanka'. In *International Journal of Epidemiology*. 2007; 36 (6): p1235.

5. Gunnell, D, Fernando, R, Hewagama, M, Priyangika, W.D.D., Konradsen, F and Eddlestone, M. 2007.

6. Centers for Disease Control and Prevention. 'National Suicide Statistics at a Glance: Case Fatality Rate Among Persons Ages Ten Years and Older for Males and Females Separately, and by Selected Mechanism for Both Sexes Combined, United States, 2005-2009.' Publication Date Unavailable (cited 16 April 2014). Available from cdc.gov/violenceprevention/suicide/statistics/case_fatality.html.

7. Okoro, C.A, Nelson, D.E., Mercy, J.A, Balluz, L.S., Crosby, A.E. and Mokdad, A.H. 'Prevalence of Household Firearms and Firearm – Storage Practices in the Fifty States and the District of Columbia: Findings from the Behavioural Risk

Factor Surveillance System 2002'. In *Pediatrics*. 2005; 116 (3): e70 -e76.

8. Miller, M., Lippmann, S.J., Azrael, D. and Hemenway, D. 'Household Firearm Ownership and Rates of Suicide Across the Fifty United States'. In *Journal of Trauma-Injury Infection and Critical Care*. 2007; 62 (4): pp1029-1035.

9. Loftin, C., McDowall, D., Wiersama, B. and Cottey, T.J. 'Effects of Restrictive Licensing of Handguns on Homicide and Suicide in the District of Columbia'. In *The New England Journal of Medicine*. 1991; 325: pp1615-20.

10. Reisch, T., Steffen, T., Habenstein, A. and Tschacher, W. 'Change in Suicide Rates in Switzerland Before and After Firearm Restriction Resulting From the 2003 "Army XXI" Reform'. In *American Journal of Psychiatry*. 2013; 170: pp977-984.

11. Simon, T.R., Swann, A.C., Powell, K.E., Potter, L.B., Kresnow, M and O'Carroll, P.W. 'Characteristics of Impulsive Suicide Attempts and Attempters'. In *Suicide and Life Threatening Behaviour*. 2002; 32 (Issue Supplement s1): pp49-59.

12. Runeson, B., Tidemalm, D., Dahlin, M., Lichtenstein, P. and Langstrom, N. 'Method of Attempted Suicide as Predictor of Subsequent Successful Suicide'. In *British Medical Journal*. 2010; 340 (C3222).

13. Andersen, S. 'The Urge to End it All'. *New York Times*. 6 July 2008 (cited 19 February 2014). Available from www.nytimes.com/2008/07/06/magazine/06suicide-t.html?pagewanted=all&_r=0.

14. Walsh, D. Interviewed by Beattie, D. 4 October 2013.

15. Oklahoma Health. 'What you Should Know about Suicide'. Publication date unavailable. (cited 18 October 2013). Available from www.ok.gov/health2/documents/CG_Suicide.pdf.

16. Holmgren, A. and Jones, A. 'Demographics of Suicide Victims in Sweden in Relation to Their Blood-alcohol Concentration and the Circumstances and Manner of Death'. In *Forensic Science International*. 2010; 198 (1-3): pp17-22; and Pridmore, S. *Suicide and Predicament: Life is a Predicament*. Bentham Science Publishers, 2010.

17. Walsh, B. and Walsh, D. 'Suicide in Ireland: The Influence of Alcohol and Unemployment'. In *Economic and Social Review*. 2011; 42 (1): pp27-47.

18. Wasserman, D., Varnik, A. and Eklund, G. 'Female Suicides and Alcohol Consumption During Perestroika in the Former USSR'. In *Acta Psychiatrica Scandinavica*. 1998; Supplement 394: pp26-27.

19. Wasserman, D., Varnik, A. and Eklund, G. 'Male suicides and alcohol consumption in the former USSR. In *Acta Psychiatrica Scandinavica*. 1994; 89: pp306-313.

20. Varnik, A., Wasserman, D., Dankowicz, M. and Eklund, G. 'Marked Decrease in Suicide Among Men and Women in the Former USSR During Perestroika'. In *Acta Psychiatrica Scandinavica*. 1998; Supplement 394: pp13-19.

21. Lester, D. 'Effect of Changing Alcohol Laws in Iceland on Suicide Rates. In *Psychological Reports*. 1999; 84 (3 pt 2): p1158.

Chapter Twelve | Suicide Prevention: What Works? | Interventions for Those at Increased Risk

1. Walsh, D. Interviewed by Beattie, D. 30 September 2013.

2. Carey, B. 'Expert on Mental Illness Reveals Her Own Fight'. *New York Times*. 23 June 2011 (cited 8 January 2014). Available from nytimes.com/2011/06/23/health/23lives. html?pagewanted=all&_r=0.

3. Carey, B. 2011.

4. Linehan M.M., Armstrong, H.E., Suarez, A., Allmon, D. and Heard, H.L. 'Cognitive-Behavioral Treatment of Chronically Parasuicidal Borderline Patients'. In *Archives of General Psychiatry*. 1991; 48(12): pp1060-64.

5. Linehan, M.M., Comtois, K.A., Murray, A.M., Brown, M.Z., Gallop, R.J., Heard. H.L. et al. 'Two-Year Randomized Controlled Trial and Follow-up of Dialectical Behavior Therapy vs Therapy by Experts for Suicidal Behaviors and Borderline Personality Disorder'. In *Archives of General Psychiatry*. 2007; 63(7): pp757-766.

6. Linehan, M.M. *Cognitive-Behavioral Treatment of Borderline Personality Disorder*. New York: Guilford Press, 1993; Dimeff, L. and Linehan, M.M. 'Dialectical Behaviour Therapy in a Nutshell'. In *The California Psychologist*. 2001; 34: pp10-13.

7. Cipriani, A, Hawton, K, Stockton, S and Geddes, J.R. 'Lithium in the Prevention of Suicide in Mood Disorders: Updated Systematic Review and Meta-analysis'. In *British Medical Journal*: 2013; 346:f3646.

8. Luxton, D.D., June, J.D. and Comtois, K.A. 'Can Post-discharge Follow-up Contacts Prevent Suicide and Suicidal Behaviour? A Review of the Evidence'. In *Crisis*. 2013; 34(1): pp32-41.

9. Fleischmann, A., Bertolote, J.M., Wasserman, D., de Leo, D., Bolhari, J., Botega, N.J. et al. 'Effectiveness of Brief Intervention and Contact for Suicide Attempters: A Randomised Controlled Trial in Five Countries'. In *Bulletin of the World Health Organization*. 2008; 86: pp703-709.

10. Stanley, B. and Brown, G.K. 'Safety Planning Intervention: A Brief Intervention to Mitigate Suicide Risk'. In *Cognitive and Behavioural Practice*. 2012; 19: pp256-64.

11. Stanley, B. and Brown, G.K. 'Safety Plan Treatment Manual to Reduce Suicide Risk: Veteran Version'. 2008 (cited 22 February 2014). Available from mentalhealth.va.gov/docs/ va_safety_planning_manual.pdf.

12. Surgenor, P. Can Men Talk If Their Lives Depend on It? Gender Differences in a Dialogue-based Suicide Intervention Programme at Pieta House, Ireland'. In *46th Annual Conference of the American Associations of Suicidology*. April 2013; Austin, Texas.

Chapter Thirteen | Summing Up Suicide Prevention

1. Carbery, G. 'Road Deaths Increase for the First Time Since 2005, Figures Show'. *Irish Times* (online). 1 January 2014 (cited 15 March 2014). Available from irishtimes.com/ news/ireland/irish-news/road-deaths-increase-for-first-time-since-2005-figures-show-1.1641377.

2. Scott, A. and Guo, B. 'For Which Strategies of Suicide Prevention Is There Evidence of Effectiveness?' Copenhagen: WHO Regional Office for Europe (Health Evidence Network report), 2012.

3. Brophy, J. Interviewed by Beattie, D. 25 March 2014.

4. Walsh, D. Interviewed by Beattie, D. 4 October 2013.

5. Gunnell, D., Fernando, R., Hewagama, M., Priyangika, W.D.D., Konradsen, F. and Eddlestone, M. 'The Impact of Pesticide Regulations on Suicide in Sri Lanka'. In *International Journal of Epidemiology*. 2007; 36 (6): p1235.

6. Manuweera, G., Eddleston, M., Egodage, S. and Buckley, N.A. 'Do Targeted Bans of Insecticides to Prevent Deaths from Self-poisoning Result in Reduced Agricultural Output?' In *Environmental Health Perspectives*. 2008; 116 (4): pp492-495.

7. Hawton, K, Fagg, J., Simkin, S., Harriss, L. and Malmberg, A. 'Methods Used for Suicide by Farmers in England and Wales. The Contribution of Availability and Its Relevance to Prevention'. In *The British Journal of Psychiatry*. 1998; 173: pp320-324.

8. Hawton, K., Bergen, H., Simkin, S., Arensman, E., Corcoran, P., Cooper, J. et al. 'Impact of Different Pack Sizes of Paracetamol in the United Kingdom and Ireland on Intentional Overdoses: A Comparative Study'. In *BMC Public Health*. 2011; 11: p460.

9. Bennewith, O., Nowers, M. and Gunnell, D. 'Effect of Barriers on the Clifton Suspension Bridge, England, on Local Patterns of Suicide: Implications for Prevention'. In *British Journal of Psychiatry*. 2007; 190: pp266-67.

10. Pelletier, A.R. 'Preventing Suicide by Jumping: The Effect of a Bridge-safety Fence'. In *Injury Prevention*. 2007; 13: pp57-59.

11. Reisch, T. and Michel, K. 'Securing a Suicide Hot Spot: Effects of a Safety Net at the Bern Muenster Terrace'. In *Suicide and Life Threatening Behaviour*. 2005; 35 (4): pp460-467.

12. Wagenaar, A.C., Salois, M.J. and Komro, K.A. 'Effects of Beverage Alcohol Price and Tax Levels on Drinking: A Meta Analysis of 1003 Estimates from 112 Studies'. In *Addiction*. 2009; 104: pp179-190.

13. Long, J. and Mongan, D. 'Alcohol Consumption in Ireland 2013: Analysis of a National Alcohol Diary Survey'. Dublin: HRB, 2014.

14. Duignan, R. Interviewed by Beattie, D. 22 November 2013.

Chapter Fourteen | Aftermath of a Suicide

1. Dyregrov, K. 'What Do We Know About Needs for Help After

Suicide in Different Parts of the World? A Phenomenological Perspective'. In *Crisis*. 2011; 32 (6): pp310-318.

2. Saarinen, P., Viinamäki, H., Hintikka, J., Lehtonen, J. and Lönnqvist, J. 'Psychological Symptoms of Close Relatives of Suicide Victims'. In *European Journal of Psychiatry*. 1999; 13: pp33-39.

3. Saarinen, P., Hintikka, J., Viinamäki, H., Lehtonen, J. and Lönnqvist, J. 'Is It Possible to Adapt to the Suicide of a Close Individual? Results of a Ten-year Prospective Follow-up Study'. In *International Journal of Social Psychiatry*. 2000; 46: pp182-90.

4. Brophy, J. Interviewed by Beattie, D. 25 March 2014.

5. Range, L.M. and Calhoun, L.J. 'Responses Following Suicide and Other Types of Death: The Perspective of the Bereaved'. In *Omega*. 1990; 21: pp311-320.

6. Range, L.M., Bright, P.S. and Ginn, P.D. 'Public Reactions to Child Suicide: Effects of Age and Method Used'. In *Journal of Community Psychology*. 1985; 13: pp288-294; and Reynolds, F.M.T. and Cimbolic, P. 'Attitudes Towards Suicide Survivors as a Function of Survivor Relationships to the Victim'. In *Omega, Journal of Death and Dying*. 1988; 19: pp125-133; and Cerel, J., Jordan, J.R. and Duberstein, P.R. 'The Impact of Suicide on the Family'. In *Crisis*. 2008; 29 (1): pp38-44.

7. Dunn, R.G. and Morrish-Vidners, D. 'The Psychological and Social Experience of Suicide Survivors'. In *Omega*. 1987-1988; 18: pp175-215; and Jordan, J.R. 'Is Suicide Bereavement Different? A Reassessment of the Literature'. In *Suicide and Life-threatening Behaviour*. 2001; 31 (1): pp91-102.

8. Wurst, F.M., Kunz, I., Skipper, G., Wolfersdorf, M., Beine, K.H. and Thon, N. 'The Therapist's Reaction to a Patient's

Suicide: Results of a Survey and Implications for Health-Care Professionals' Well-being'. In *Crisis*. 2011; 32 (2): pp99-105.

9. Murray, D. Interviewed by Beattie, D. 30 September 2013.

10. Brophy, J. 2014.

11. Brophy, J. 2014.

12. Ting, L., Sanders, S., Jacobson, J.M. and Power, J.R. 'Dealing with the Aftermath: A Qualitative Analysis of Mental-Health Social Workers' Reactions after a Client Suicide'. In *Social Work*. 2006; 51 (4): pp329-41.

13. Ting, L., Sanders, S., Jacobson, J.M. and Power, J.R. 2006.